Cabins

Cabins

ESCAPE TO NATURE

images
Publishing

Contents

vipp

On the frontier: the cabin in the 21st century

By Damon Hayes Couture

On the frontier

The cabins found within this book give new form to an old idea. While they may not look like the rustic cabins of the past, they share a similar essence: they exist on the frontier. The cabin was once a pragmatic solution to the need for shelter on the frontier of settlement. It has now also become an architectural exploration of the frontier and of what it means to design, build, and live in the twenty-first century. The idea of the cabin exists between these two definitions—the limit of settled land, beyond which lies wilderness, and the limit of understanding, beyond which lies another kind of wilderness.

The notion of the cabin blurs the boundaries between dream and reality, inspiration and experimentation, tradition and technology, and nature and culture. Following a narrative of dreaming of the cabin, drawing the cabin, building the cabin, and living in the cabin, we will see how the contemporary cabin exists at the frontier of architectural exploration.

A daydream of departure

The cabin has a captivating presence in the landscapes of our daydreams. In our reveries, we might imagine reaching an alpine hut after a steep ascent up a mountainside or happening upon a secluded shelter on the trail through a quiet forest. Seeking both adventure and tranquility, our collective wanderlust has led to a resurgence in interest about cabins. While the cabin's coordinates on each of our mental maps may vary, the feeling remains the same—an island of comfort and calm isolated in an inspiring landscape. It might be a familiar place that we return to with our family and friends, a foreign place we dream of traveling to someday, or a fictional place we visit only in our thoughts. Whether real or imagined, the cabin appeals to our desire to escape from our urban surroundings and retreat into nature. In a lucid daydream, the cabin stands as a distant landmark in our imaginations, just beyond the horizon, inviting us to go and explore.

More than just a shelter to retreat to, the cabin also offers the prospect of living differently, whether by living with less or living closer to nature. In preparing for a trip to the cabin, we take only what is necessary, and packing is accompanied by a sense of restless anticipation. Finally, with everything strategically sorted and packed, we set off toward the cabin.

The journey to the cabin is a transformative experience that offers us a different perspective on the landscape and our lives within it. On the main road out of the city, the highrises of downtown are seen from a new vantage point, diminishing into the horizon until they disappear from view. Billboards give way to trees, concrete buildings to rock formations, and highway traffic to wildlife. From the linear trajectory of the highway, the route to the cabin evolves into a zig-zagging path down backroads. Whether traveling through a field, in a forest, up a mountain, or along the ocean, the landscape takes hold and directs our path. The journey to the cabin traces our trail to the frontier between urban density and nature.

Names for the cabin

The cabin goes by many names. Whether a camp, cottage, hut, lodge, shack, shed, or shelter, we use the synonyms of cabin to express its geographic diversity and formal variety. The Swiss refer to a mountain cabin as a chalet, the Norwegians call a cabin on the farm a *sœter,* and the idiosyncratic islanders of Cape Breton, Canada, refer to a summer cabin as a bungalow. The breadth of cultures that have a tradition of building and visiting cabins is a testament to its universal practicality and appeal.

The many names for cabin express a shared tradition of seeking out the frontier. More than simply wood, concrete, and steel, cabins are imbued with past and present cultural values and communicate our relationship to the landscape. As Norwegian historian of technology and environment, Finn Arne Jørgensen writes, cabins "are as much ideas as actual places; they are observation points outside of time and space from which we can observe not just nature but ourselves and the world we live in."[1] The cabin, after all, is not just a private building out in the wilderness somewhere, it is part of a shared cultural narrative, a collection of ideas that has developed over time.

1 Finn Arne Jørgensen, "Why look at Cabin Porn?," in *Public Culture,* vol. 27, no. 3 (United States: Duke University Press, 2015), pp. 557–78.

Origins of the cabin

Like many architectural typologies, the cabin has an indefinite form with as many variations as there are landscapes and materials. Found in building vernaculars throughout the world, the cabin has undergone many practical transformations and spatial configurations: from the temporary camps of settler expansion, to lodging for workers who built the infrastructure that connected continents, from holiday homes for the emerging middle class to rentals for short-term stays. The complex history of the cabin and its enduring appeal in contemporary culture is what makes the building typology an intriguing topic to explore.

The exact origins of the cabin are unknown. Imagining a hypothetical past, early modern architectural theorist, Marc-Antoine Laugier speculates that the cabin is the origin of architecture itself, as he describes a process of using fallen branches to create a rudimentary cabin.[2] While Laugier's thought experiment may not pinpoint the exact origins of the cabin, it informs us of the cabin's role as an essential building typology.

With the rise of tourism in Europe during the mid-nineteenth century came a significant change in the way people, especially the urban elite, interacted with nature. The Romantic movement popularized the pursuit of exploring nature to experience "the sublime," the feeling of awe we experience in the face of nature's immensity and beauty. On the Romantic wanderers' forays into nature the cabin itself became a point of fascination. Cabin-goers channel their legacy even during a weekend getaway. Between sunbathing and jigsaw puzzles, the desire to connect to a picturesque beauty remains a part of every visit to the cabin.

Destiny, manifested

At the same time as the growing leisure class was enjoying the last vestiges of European wilderness, illustrations of homesteads on the North American frontier were enticing Europeans to colonize the New World. Whether the settlers were from Scandinavia or Eastern Europe, they brought their building traditions with them. Still on the move, the settlers built basic log cabins, hewn from freshly felled timbers. Despite its rustic and rudimentary provisions, or maybe because of them, the log cabin remains a constant source of inspiration for contemporary cabin-goers.

After the initial wave of expansion into the frontier, settlers pushed further into the wilderness to build the infrastructure that would power and connect the North American continent. Loggers, miners, and railroad workers, among laborers in many other trades,

2 Marc-Antoine Laugier, *An Essay on Architecture* (original French 1753), trans. Wolfgang and Anni Herrmann (Los Angeles: Hennesey & Ingalls, 1977), pp. 11–12.

required basic shelter while performing their demanding jobs. Many of the early workers' cabins began as tent houses—timber-framed and canvas-clad structures that were meant to be as impermanent and transitory as the workers who lived in them. With a translucent canvas skin, the cabins glowed from within, illuminating the surrounding forest like a lantern. As settlement patterns solidified, some tent houses became a permanent fixture on the landscape and were often upgraded long after their initial construction. Walls were framed in, wood flooring was constructed over the hardened dirt, weather-tight roofs were added, wood stoves were installed, and sometimes even electrical wiring was strung through the walls. The incremental process of building a tent house over many seasons reflects the way that many self-builders and "weekend warriors" build their cabins today.

Getting away

After the post-war housing boom of the twentieth century, both mainstream and counterculture in North America became equally enamored with the cabin, albeit for very different reasons. With all the conveniences of modern life available to them in their urban and suburban surroundings, the emerging middle class turned their attention toward building vacation homes in nature. Magazines presented low-cost, do-it-yourself cabins as "the answer to everybody's dream: a place to get away from it all for as little money as possible."[3] Recognizing an opportunity, the construction industry used the cabin as a way of prototyping new materials and technologies, which they then marketed to the masses. These bold new cabins, including the newly developed A-frame, had a broad appeal in society, which continues today, albeit with a distinctively retro charm.

At the same time, the 1960s counterculture was experimenting with radically new living arrangements. In communes such as Drop City, Colorado, forward-thinking architects and hippies built novel structures that, to varying degrees of sophistication, presented a striking departure from building traditions and social conventions. The innovations they developed—ways of using recycled products as building materials, and earth-building techniques—were documented and shared in publications. This movement's impact on the idea of the cabin and its promise of escape and transcendence remains. The contemporary off-the-grid, tiny house, and DIY movements that are gaining in popularity today owe much to their 1960s predecessors' architectural innovations and their bold spirit of self-reliance. Many of the cabins included in this book, such as Ark-Shelter (page 134) are off-the-grid, self-sustaining, and eco-friendly, allowing their placement in the most remote of locations.

3 "Vacation Cabin," *Woman's Day*, August 1958, p. 17.

Contemporary cabin culture

The busier our lives become and the more technologically connected we are, the more the lure of the cabin as a retreat grows. The secluded cabin in nature is often prescribed as the antidote to the stress of modern life, if only to quarantine ourselves from encroaching technology.

As our appetite to escape the presence of technology increases, the more the cabin appears on our social media feeds. Images of cabins have become a kind of digital escapism, a small dose of the experience we crave. Finn Arne Jørgensen remarks that, "The images seem to say that we once lived in simpler conditions, in architecture closer to nature ... The images of cabin porn whisper to us of this lost state of grace, of an age of wood and earth and things that were real and true."[4] Rather than a substitute for the experience, images of cabins are part of it, conditioning our expectations and contributing to our stock of dreams.

Technology has made cabins more accessible than ever. Online short-term rentals services make the dream of staying in the cabin accessible at the click of a button. The enticing images allow us to imagine a different way of life and if we're lucky enough to visit, explore its potential. CABN "Jude" (page 272), set in Australia's picturesque Adelaide Hills, not only offers a respite from the modern way of life, but actively encourages disengaging from modern technology such as smart phones.

Dreaming of the cabin

A cabin always begins as a dream. Sometimes fantastical and sometimes familiar, the dream is the indispensable starting point to any journey to the cabin. By visiting the cabin, we are able to transform our everyday experience and participate in a collective cultural narrative. More than simply a solitary experience, the image of the cabin we have in our mind's eye is a product of our culture, a shared idea of place. Founding myths, literary references, and artistic allusions are all part of the cabin's meaningful connection to the collective cultural narrative. The cabin, therefore, is an expressive medium that can convey complex concepts about the transformation of space and the meaning of place. The cabins of this book exist on the frontier between dream and reality.

When we reach the cabin at dusk and survey the land, the cabin outline is barely discernible from its surroundings. From a distance, the cabin is an integral part of the landscape and, as we participate in the scene, we become part of it as well. Whether by exertion or by imagination, reaching the cabin is both a refuge and a reward.

4 Finn Arne Jørgensen, "Why look at Cabin Porn?," in *Public Culture,* vol. 27, no. 3 (United States: Duke University Press, 2015), pp. 557–78.

Dreams to playful reality

When the sun slowly rises and the snow melts away after a long winter, the people of Scandinavia, perhaps more than any other region, are ready to spend their summers at the cabin. Bordering on a national obsession, the Finns have an unparalleled cabin culture thanks in part to the pioneering designs of Alvar Aalto.

Alvar Aalto's architectural career, which spanned the mid-century modernist period, is defined as much by his relentless pursuit of modernist principles as it is his deep connection to the culture and climate of Scandinavia. In examining the region's vernacular, Aalto remarked that the Karelian log cabins of Finland parallel the collection of Finnish founding myths collected in the *Kalevala*. Isolated from outside influence, the region's people produced buildings whose construction was dictated directly by the natural conditions, and described by Aalto as "a forest architecture pure and simple."[5] By tapping into the national founding mythology of the Finnish people, Aalto reminds us of the importance of a shared cultural narrative as the locus of all regionalist design.

5 Randall Thomas and Trevor Garnham, *The Environments of Architecture: Environmental Design in Context* (Abingdon, United Kingdom: Taylor & Francis, 2007), p. 43.

The Muuratsalo Experimental House was Aalto's studio and summer home, on which he worked for decades, allowing him to transform it over time and test new ideas. For Aalto, Muuratsalo was a kind of a laboratory for architecture, where they followed his oft repeated maxim: "Don't forget to play."

The Garden House (page 280) is a dream-like cabin that simply and playfully evokes the idea of transformation. At first glance, it looks like an unassuming garden shed on a picturesque pond. As designer and builder Caspar Schols describes the cabin, it is a hybrid building "between an umbrella and a suitcase." As if by magic, the cabin has the ability to change based on the weather of the day and the season of the year. Channeling Aalto's maxim, Schols did not forget to play in designing and building the Garden House.

To the unsuspecting passerby, Antoine (page 126) appears to be just another rock on the steep slopes of the Alps. As in our dreams, however, what initially appears to be a mundane encounter, can quickly transform into a mythical experience. As a tribute to the alpine experience, Antoine abounds with references to the geography and culture of the Alps. Rife with literary and artistic references, Antoine by BUREAU shows that the simple cabin can have a narrative dimension and tell the story of a place. Similar to the ethos of Alvar Aalto, but radically different in form, Antoine manifests the myths of the place to give shape to the cabin.

Drawing the cabin

We have all traced the outline of a cabin. Resembling a child's drawing, the small dwelling with its gabled roof is the familiar symbol of the cabin and is instantly inviting. As with many of the cabins found within this book, like Folly (page 140) or Island House (page 262), the gabled form serves as an elemental building block, the symbolic origin of the cabin. Of course, the simple elevation just described isn't the only starting point for the design of the cabin. Designers can take inspiration by walking the site to understand the lay of the land, making a model of the roof to develop a form, imagining the flow of experiences to sort out the program, or studying the surrounding trees to get a sense of the appropriate materials. Once the seed of an idea, the concept, has been planted, the design can grow and take shape according to the daylight and views. With all these considerations in mind and many more, the cabin is given its form. A drawing of the cabin, whether drawn by hand or printed on paper, gives the idea of a different way of life.

For architects, the appeal of the cabin is in the clarity of the brief: basic, temporary shelter. Given this simple program and its small scale, the cabin invites experimentation with siting, form, program, and materials. In drawing and redrawing the cabin, designers have the freedom to radically reinterpret the typology and give new form to an old idea. Examples may range from the petite Urban Cabin (page 286) or the enterprising DD16 (page 256), mounted on pontoons on a lake. Architects have used the cabin as a testing ground for ideas and some have made it into a physical manifesto, a tangible declaration of their architectural theories. From Marcus Vitruvius and Mark-Antoine Laugier to Frank Lloyd Wright and Le Corbusier, the cabin has been on the frontier of architectural exploration for centuries, and continues to provide room for experimentation and discovery, as architects experiment with different materials and forms of insulation, as seen in the COBS Year-Round Micro Cabins (page 56). The lines connecting dream and reality, inspiration and experimentation, tradition and technology, nature and culture are drawn and mediated through design.

Drawing and organic architecture

Perhaps no other architect is more closely associated with the quintessential architectural activity of drawing than Frank Lloyd Wright. Whether on the drafting table or on the back of a postcard, his evocative sketches have a visionary clarity of intention. With a few deft strokes, his drawings carry the meaning of the architectural language he developed over his lifetime.

In the Sonoma Desert, Wright founded his home, studio, garden sanctuary, and laboratory for architecture: Taliesin West. It took four years to build, and then Wright immediately started making changes. On his regular rambles around the site, he traced a trail on the desert as if tracing a line on a page. By incrementally adapting to the landscape, the various iterations of Taliesin West embody Wright's ideas of organic architecture. Wright believed that a building should be intimately connected to a particular moment and a specific landscape, as if growing naturally out of the ground. While perhaps not growing naturally out of the ground, ORIGIN Tree House (page 46) with its almost organic form certainly shows similarities with its inspiration: a birds' nest, and provides an intimate connection to its location high in the trees.

Adapting to the landscape

Built on the site of the family cabin where Mark Erickson, principal at Studio North, and his family have been returning to for decades, the Birdhut (page 42) is shaped by a knowledge of and curiosity about the ecology of the forest. A longstanding interest in the local ecology led the designer to create a more intimate encounter beyond passive observation. Birdhut explores the idea of cohabitation between people and wildlife, where they become roommates in a way. People inhabit the structure for a short time, the rest of the time the Birdhut belongs to the forest. Between inspiration and experimentation, the Birdhut shows that the cabin is constantly being reinterpreted.

Building the cabin

In an effort to unite tradition and technology, designers and builders have reinterpreted the cabin typology to develop new ways of practicing architecture and new ways of building, and as a result are able to extend the places where a structure may be constructed, even on a wintry mountain in the Slovenian Alps. The cabins of this book exist on the frontier between tradition and technology.

Building the cabin is an incremental process where we gradually reconcile the conditions of the site with the dream in our heads and the drawings on paper. Whether concrete or stone, the foundations are the first to go in. Once a solid connection to the ground is established (and this may include anchor lines, particularly on the more precarious sites) and we become anchored to the site, the floor is framed. Taking the initial steps on the open platform gives us the chance, perhaps for the first time, to experience what it is like to walk through the space. As the walls are tilted into place, the cabin becomes enclosed and takes on its final form. When the openings of the windows are punctured through the facade, we are presented with framed views through to the landscape beyond, perhaps capturing a view of a nearby mountain or a glimpse of a stand of trees. Although the roofs of today might be more robust than the branches of Laugier's Primitive Hut, the roof fulfils its essential role of providing shelter from the elements, even extreme snow load weights or high winds. Always a work in progress, the rustic nature of the cabin presents the ideal opportunity to experiment with the space as we begin to use it. Things are allowed, if not encouraged, to be rough around the edges and show the signs of the hands that worked on it and the time that aged it. The Japanese refer to it as "wabi-sabi," the beauty of imperfection and change, as seen expressed by the Shelter for the Wanderer cabin (page 156) in Chile which of necessity was constructed with salvaged materials, and retains a very rough and rustic appearance.

Building a cabin is about more than the satisfaction of hammering two-by-fours together until a building takes form, but about tapping into a feeling of connectedness to place and community. Whether stacking timbers to make a log cabin or stacking stones to build a fire pit, there is enjoyment to be found in the effort itself. Building a cabin is done for its own sake, for the experience of creation. The mystique associated with the self-built cabin, from Henry David Thoreau's cabin on Walden Pond to the A-frame constructed from a kit of parts, is enduring. By building by hand and on-site we become acquainted with the site's unique characteristics.

The self-built cabin is rarely realized in isolation, however, even if it is often thought of as an essay in self-sufficiency. Even on the frontier, the construction of the log cabin was a product of community cooperation. Whether built on-site or prefabricated in parts, the process works best as a collaborative experience, even if that is a joining of efforts by designers from different countries, as the partnership behind the design for Alpine Shelter Skuta (page 102) cabin demonstrates.

Living deliberately in the cabin

Forever associated with cabin lore, Henry David Thoreau's self-built cabin at Walden Pond in Concord, Massachusetts, is an essay in self-sufficiency. Thoreau's experiment in "living deliberately" is an attempt to transcend the conventions of society by building the most basic requirements of living: shelter. As a proto how-to guide, Thoreau describes his education in building in step-by-step detail. Included among the philosophical passages about the virtues of living independent of society's conventions, are prosaic passages about the process, materials, and budget of building his cabin. Ever since he constructed his small cabin beside Walden Pond and narrated his experiences, his readers have been rushing to repeat his feat. Advances in architectural design and modern materials have made it easier to adopt an off-the-grid and self-sufficient lifestyle.

By leaving society and living in solitude, Thoreau makes the ultimate commitment to self-reliance. According to Ralph Waldo Emerson, Thoreau's benefactor and mentor, self-reliance is a practical ideal that combines metaphysical philosophy with tangible know-how. For the Transcendentalists, as they referred to themselves, it isn't enough to simply dream up theories, one has to live them out. Channeling the Roman thinker Seneca, Ralph Waldo Emerson captures the ethos of building, "The reward of a thing done well is to have done it."

Collaborative dreaming

Spearheaded by Matthew Kennedy of Studio North, Dream/Dive Platform (page 64) was built as a collaborative weekend project at the family cabin. Made out of "salvaged materials from under the deck, supplemented with two-by-four lumber from the local hardware store," the structure was built in a few short summer days at the end of August. Having to contend only with the lay of the land, the structure cleverly makes use of the stones from the site as its structure. Dream/Dive demonstrates a design ethos of treading gently on the earth while simultaneously enjoying the process of building. In its playful experimentation, Dream/Dive shows the value in being able to both dream up ideas and then make them a reality through a collaborative building process.

Remote prefabrication

With its razor-sharp form, innovative use of materials, and remote location, the Alpine Shelter Skuta (page 102) sets a new standard for what prefabricated buildings can look like. Despite its minimal footprint, the shelter required a sizable team of more than sixty participants, including students at the Harvard Graduate School of Design, two architecture firms, and the Slovenian Armed Forces. The harsh climatic conditions introduced a veritable mountain of challenges for the architects, engineers, and installers. Within a context of extreme risk, every aspect of the project was meticulously thought-out and executed. The shelter consists of three structurally robust frames that allow for ease of transport as well as divide the space according to the intended uses. The installation of the shelter was carried out by helicopter transport with the Slovenian Armed Forces and a team of mountaineers from the Mountain Rescue Service. DublDom Kandalaksha (page 78) is another example of a prefabricated module design that is readily adapted to an extreme environment. Prefabricated cabin structures have been popular in the past, and the updated modern module constructions show the way of the future.

Living in the cabin

Having dreamed of the journey to the cabin, drawn it in its surroundings, and built it with the available means and materials, we have yet to live inside the cabin, which is an art in itself. Spending the calm and solitude of an afternoon in the cabin makes all the steps in the journey even more worth their while.

The cabin can be a place of long-term dwelling, where a meaningful connection to the space and place is gained through the passage of time. It can also be a one-time getaway, where quotidian life is momentarily traded for a spectacular experience. Whether as a family tradition or a short-term stay, a visit to the cabin allows us to become acquainted with another life in another place, even if only temporarily.

On the frontier between nature and culture, the appeal of the cabin lies in the rituals of living closer to nature and living with less. At the cabin, we do things for their own sake. The simplicity of purpose at the cabin serves as a remedy to the excesses of contemporary life and as a necessary counterpoint to the intensity inherent in our digitally connected world. Our material possessions are pared down to the essentials and as such we connect to nature, time, and ourselves in a different way.

Living on the outside

For nearly two decades, French-Swiss architect Le Corbusier spent every summer at the Cabanon, his getaway in Roquebrune-Cap-Martin, France. Le Corbusier is perhaps best known for his sweeping gestures of urban razing and renewal, which makes him an unlikely pioneer of the cabin. Far from his utopian urban proposals, Le Corbusier retreated to the Mediterranean coast, where he lived in his Cabanon, a structure that resembles a traditional log cabin from the exterior, but comprises a single plywood-lined room in the interior with a spartan design.

Since the Cabanon was a minimally appointed space, Le Corbusier spent much of his time outdoors, experiencing the beauty of the Cote d'Azure. The garden around the Cabanon is a natural extension of the dwelling. The space of the dwelling is bigger than the cabin itself, extending far beyond the plywood walls of the Cabanon and out into the sea.

Living in nature

On the Hawaiian island of Maui, Erin Moore, principal of FLOAT, poetically explores the concept of living not just closer to nature, but directly in nature. Outside House (page 242), comprises two pavilions that straddle a three-hundred-year-old lava flow, one pavilion for sleeping and working and the other for cooking and eating. By placing the two pavilions at a distance from each other, the owner is forced to travel between them, making the exterior as much a part of the house as the interior. The two modest pavilions shape the basic rituals of daily life, but the interstitial space between them, allows the owner to live out an intentional relationship with the land.

Bjarke Ingels and Søren Rose, the designers of the Klein A45 cabin (page 34), shared the same daydream—as urban transplants in New York City, the Scandinavian designers shared a mutual need for a countryside escape. While they were on a road trip together to the Catskill Mountains, they conceived of an A-frame with a uniquely Scandinavian aesthetic. Like the first A-frame designs of the 1950s and 1960s, A45 is a prefabricated and flat-pack design that attempts to tap into a market that is looking for a direct connection with nature. Klein A45 is a product of its time, in line with the current movement for environmentally conscious design and the trend toward downsizing possessions. By living with less, Ingles and Rose hope, cabin goers will be able to commune with nature.

A daydream of arrival

While they may not look like the rustic log cabins of the past, the cabins found in this book share a similar essence: they exist on the frontier. From shapeshifting cabins seemingly carved out of the mountainside, to treetop perches for both birds and people, from a lakeside platform for dreaming and diving to a pair of pavilions that straddle a lava flow, the cabins in this book are experiments in how to dream, draw, build, and live differently. While its only task is to provide basic shelter, the cabin allows for something much greater: the possibility for the world outside to connect with the world within.

Damon Hayes Couture is a designer and builder with Studio North based out of Calgary, Canada. The firm's work has been included in a growing number of local and international publications, such as *Canadian Architect,* archdaily, and *Dwell.* Damon is passionate about architecture that is contemporary, while being respectful of history, and forward-looking to the challenges and opportunities of the future.
Closer to home, Damon has designed cabins for clients in the Rocky Mountains and is currently designing an addition to his family's cabin for his parents to live in during their retirement.

Autumn reflections, New York State, United States

Forest

Observe the wildlife and be at one with nature through the changing colors of the seasons by taking refuge in an innovatively designed cabin that's hidden within the dense and verdant forest greenery and under a thick canopy of trees.

A shelter for all seasons

Casa R is a tranquil family refuge set on a mountain in the Andes in southern Chile. Located near to local attractions, nature reserves and national parks, it provides an ideal base for trekking and outdoor sports. This compact yet durable structure is designed to withstand its mercurial environment, from sweltering heat to extreme cold.

The cabin has been deliberately placed on a remote site, orientated north toward the river valley. Casa R is designed to sit neatly on the natural sloping terrain, reducing costly extra foundation work, and a large part of the structure is elevated above the ground to minimize the disturbance to the landscape. The roof is steeply gabled to protect the building from any accumulation of snowfall.

The cabin includes a *chiflonera,* common in Patagonian homes, which acts as a buffer zone between the interior and exterior of the home to rebuff the cold or hot temperatures. The first floor contains the woodshed, and access to the cabin, which brings you to a compact kitchen and bathroom, and ends in the combined living/dining room, with the terrace beyond, and a spectacular view of the valley through the large window, unimpeded by trees. A spiral staircase leads to the upper level, where the bedroom, living room, and work area are located. Designed by Felipe Lagos Novoa, Casa R can not only withstand the harsh elements of its location, but is also easy to maintain.

CASA R (2018), Vilches, Chile

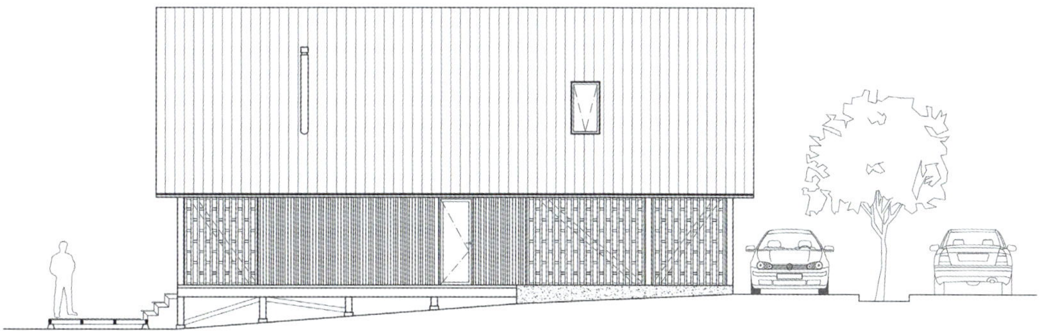

West section

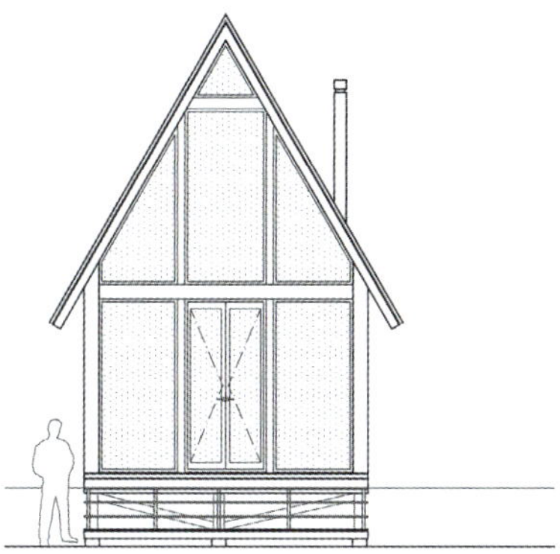

North elevation

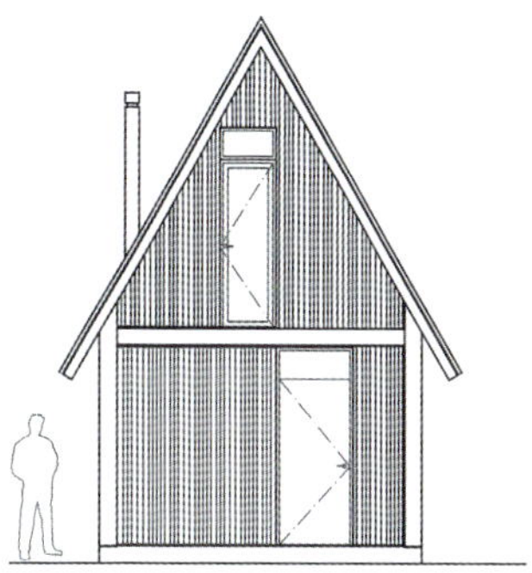

South elevation

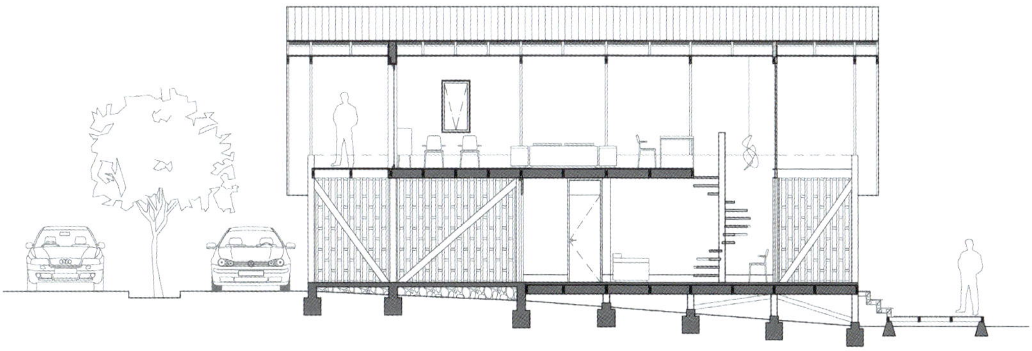

Section

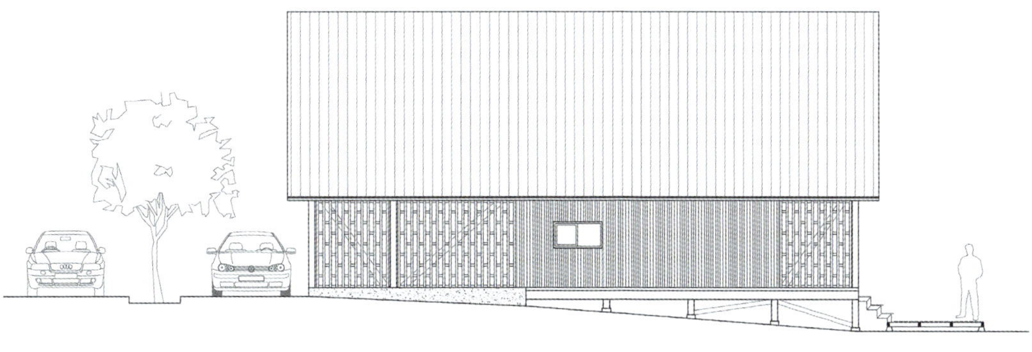

East elevation

Nordic design

The design of this traditional A-frame structure, known for its pitched roof and angled walls for easy rain run-off, has evolved into a stunning crystal-like shape. To maximize the qualities of this classic structure, Klein A45 comprises a more usable floor area: it takes the square base and twists the roof 45 degrees to raise the tiny home to a soaring 13 feet (4 meters). A triangular floor-to-ceiling window, featuring seven glass pieces, allows natural daylight to illuminate the interiors, with the resulting faceted shape giving the cabin an ever-changing appearance. Inside, the space reflects a minimal Nordic home that is prioritized for *hyggelig* comfort and design. Made entirely from recyclable materials, from the exposed timber frame in solid pine, the cedar-wood bathroom, the Douglas fir floor and customizable space-grade, insulating natural cork walls, this cabin brings nature inside. An elegant Morsøe wood-burning fireplace is nestled in one corner while off-the-grid equipment is tucked away in the back. A petite kitchen designed by Københavns Møbelsnedkeri, handcrafted furniture from Carl Hansen, and a bed fitted with Kvadrat fabric designed by Soren Rose Studio are some of the beautifully tailored Nordic flourishes that adorn the cabin.

KLEIN A45 (2018), Upstate New York, United States

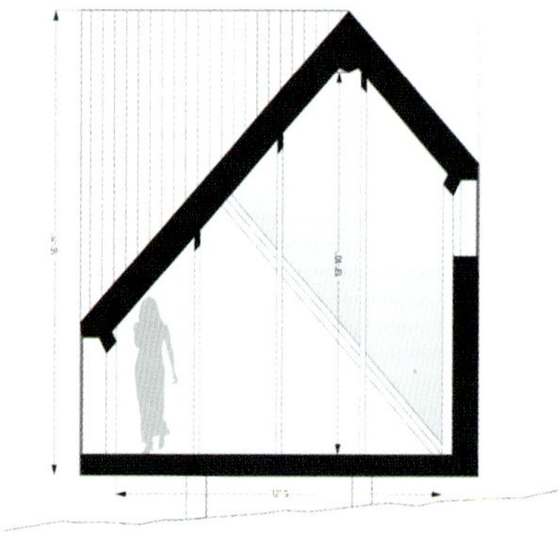

Section B

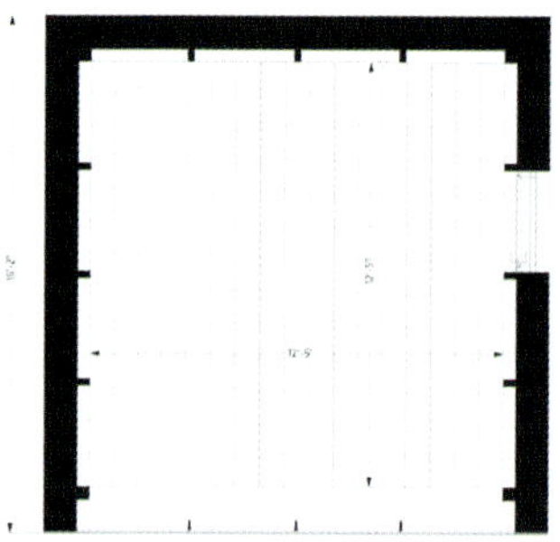

Floor plan

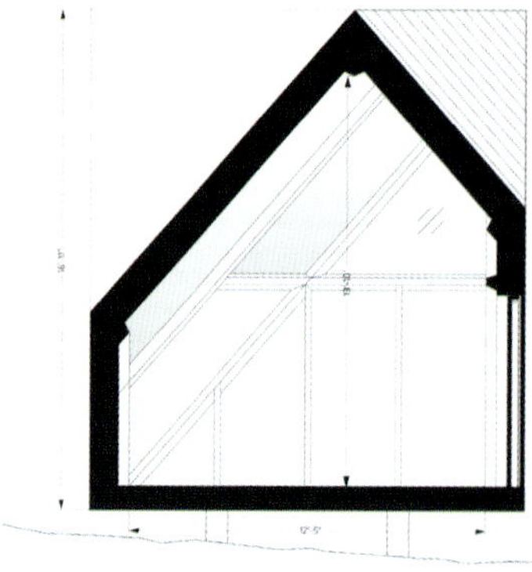

Section A

Feathered facade

Designed by Studio North, the Birdhut is a whimsical human-sized birdhouse perched high in the forest canopy, and can accommodate two people and one dog. The interior contains enough space to comfortably fit a double bed and a small living area. In addition to being an inviting place for people to nest, the shingle facade has twelve birdhouses, each designed to offer nesting opportunities for as wide a variety of local birds as possible. Mimicking the process of a bird building a nest, the materials of the Birdhut were scavenged from the immediate surroundings.

The hut is nestled in a cross-braced structure built of lodgepole pines foraged from a nearby forest that had been ravaged by fire, and sits on wooden stilts 9 feet (2.7 meters) off the ground, with its peak at 20 feet (6 meters). The platform and cladding for the hut is made of planks reclaimed from an old cabin deck. The front is clad with western red cedar shingles cut with a custom rounded profile, reminiscent of a birdhouse. The roof is made from clear polycarbonate panels, which intensifies the sense of being in the tree canopy, while also allowing the interior to be passively heated by the sun. The inside is ventilated by two portholes that punctuate the facade and the entry. A bridge connects the Birdhut to the hillside and a stone path leads down to a natural spring and campfire.

BIRDHUT (2017), Windermere, British Columbia, Canada

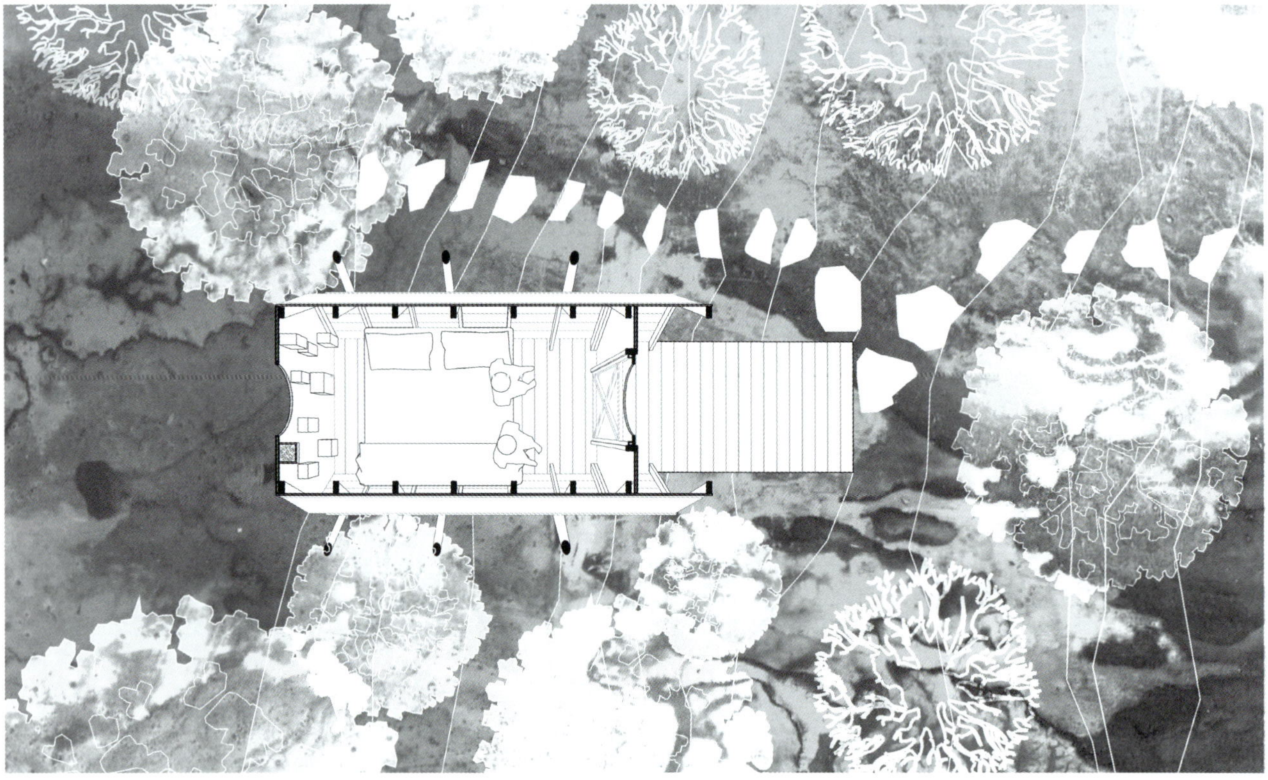

Plan

A bird in the nest

ORIGIN is an exceptional cabin, and is wrapped around a hundred-year-old oak tree, forming what the design team has termed "a tailored wooden-dress." This incredible bird-nest-like structure was indeed inspired by a bird's nest. The cabin is accessed via a walkway suspended 33 feet (10 meters) above the ground, from a platform located on another old oak tree.

Two sliding glass doors provide access from the protected patio to the interior of the structure. A wooden ladder invites visitors to continue the ascent, in close contact with the tree, to find a large 360-degree panoramic roof-terrace. The inner lining of the walls is made out of poplar, a light and clear wood with a subtle scent. The smooth, flat interior walls are matched by the custom-made furniture surfaces, worked with fine horizontal slats, in a simple game of geometric volumes. The living spaces develop in succession around the patio: from the entrance to the living area and the sleeping area, until a narrow corridor with three sliding doors that give access respectively to a dressing room, a well-equipped bathroom, and a technical closet. Each of the living spaces has a large window overlooking the forest, offering a mid-air view of the foliage of the surrounding centennial oaks.

ORIGIN TREE HOUSE (2017), Château de Raray, France

Elevation

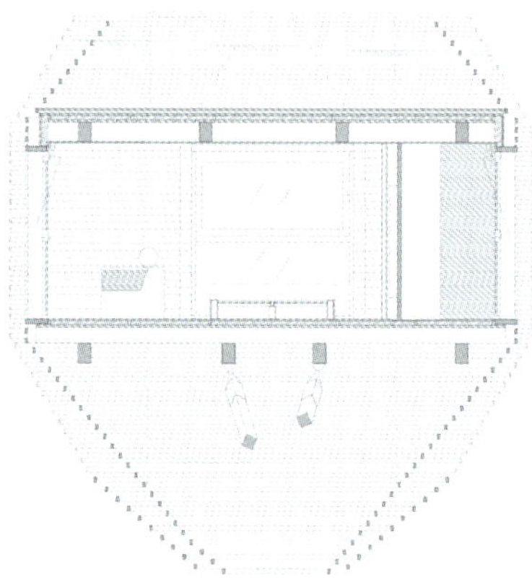

Section

Outward bound

Located deep within a pine forest, these seven all-season cabins were designed by students from Colorado Building Workshop, in association with the Colorado Outward Bound School (COBS), and are used as a base camp for outdoor education programs.

The structures are lifted off the ground by short metal columns implanted into concrete footings, thereby minimizing the visual and environmental impact of the building, and helping it to blend into the surrounding forest. The exterior is skinned with sheets of hot-rolled steel, forming a low-maintenance rainscreen. Inspired by quinzees, a snow shelter made from a hollowed-out pile of snow, the students adapted the logic of "snow insulation" for their structures. The cabins employ structurally insulated panels (SIPs) for the walls and flat roofs. The roofs are designed to hold a heavy snow load in the winter.

Each cabin contains 200 square feet (19 square meters) of interior space with a cedar-clad 100-square-foot (9-square-meter) deck surrounding the structure. No two cabins are alike, as their orientation and articulation are each unique to their immediate site conditions. The cabin interiors are clad in birch plywood bringing warmth to the structure and evoking a connection with the trees surrounding the site.

COBS YEAR-ROUND MICRO CABINS (2016), Colorado, United States

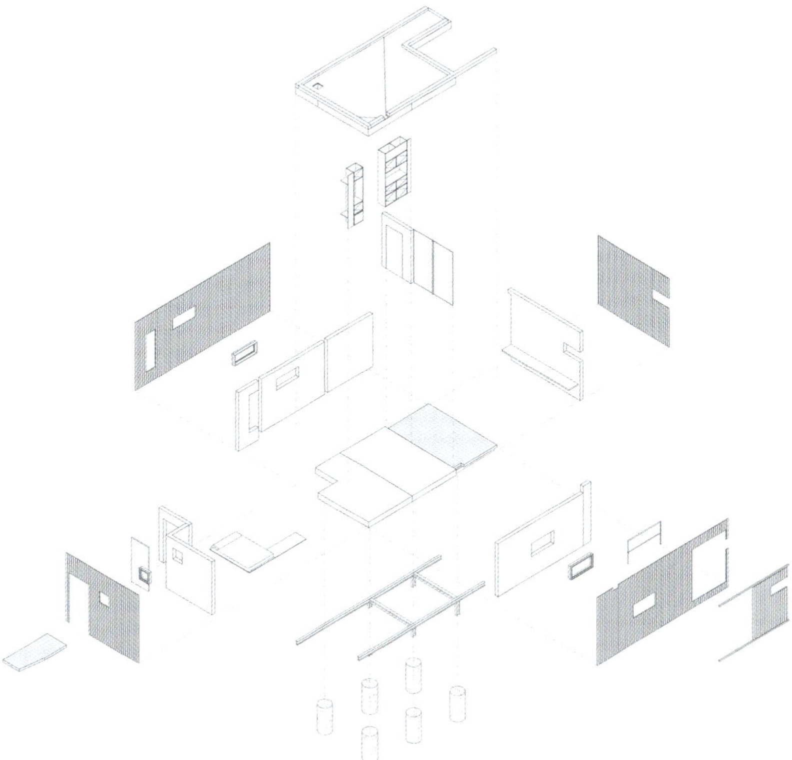

Exploded axonometric

Platform of dreams

Your environment can shape the way you think. Whether you are a child or an adult, spaces can engage your imagination, broaden your mind and excite your spirit. This dreaming platform was a collaborative weekend project at the family cottage. The screened-in hut is the new favorite spot for stargazing on beautiful summer nights and the cantilevered diving platform replaces the need for coffee in the morning!

The Dream/Dive Platform, dreamt up by Studio North, is a modest structure that sits lightly on the landscape. It simply rests on a large granite boulder and cantilevers out over the lake while the sleeping hut is pushed toward the back of the platform, and tethered to a stack of rocks, which acts as a counterweight and anchor.

The dreaming platform was constructed of salvaged materials, supplemented with lumber from the local hardware store. The basic form is a result of available materials and tools and a need for a better entry point in to the lake for swimmers. Normally swimmers would have to navigate down a rocky coastline to find a way to jump in. The structure was stripped down to its essentials to support two elemental functions, sleeping and play. A simple waxed canvas is unrolled over the hut for when the weather gets gnarly.

DREAM/DIVE PLATFORM (2015), Bobs Lake, Ontario, Canada

Dutch homage

Nestled in the verdant Noorderpark in Utrecht, the Netherlands, this off-grid cabin provides a warm and dry escape in inclement weather for the wet and tired volunteers who maintain the park. The cabin replaces a 1966 storage and break shelter for park maintenance, and continues to serve the original function, but with a modern and sleek update.

The 377-square-foot (35-square-meter) cabin was inspired by Henry David Thoreau, one of history's most revered nature lovers, and his famous cabin at Walden Pond. You can almost picture Thoreau writing *Walden* here. Hidden in the forest and covered by lush foliage during summer, the building has been shaped so that it reveals its presence only at the very last moment. Two large sliding doors open up the entire corner of the building in warmer weather, blending the interior with the surrounding open space.

At the heart of the cabin is the sculptural fireplace, providing necessary warmth during the winter months. It and the small kitchen are fueled by local firewood. The hearth supports a folding aluminum-clad roof structure, which creates a protective yet open canopy that blends into the surrounding flora. The interior is clad in warm wooden paneling, creating a rustic ambiance with minimalist tones. Overall, the cabin is modest and simple, combining a restful retreat with being in nature, just as Thoreau would appreciate.

THOREAU'S CABIN (2013), Utrecht, the Netherlands

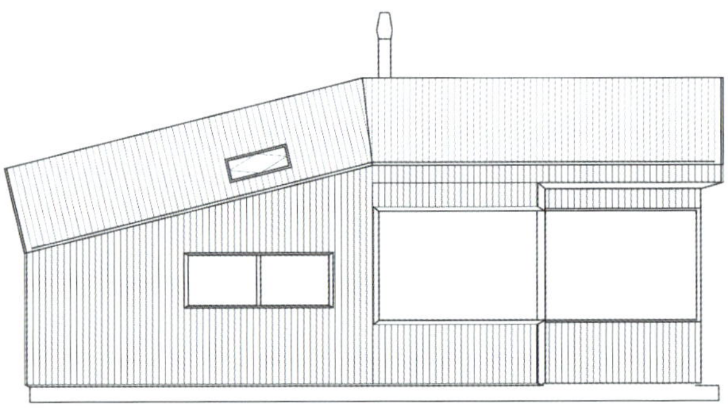

North elevation

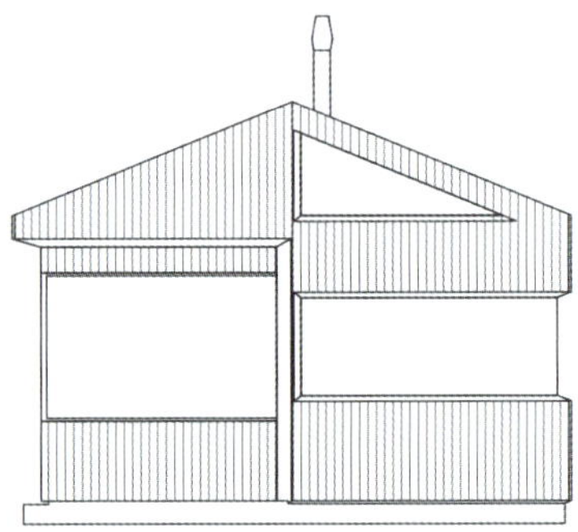

West elevation

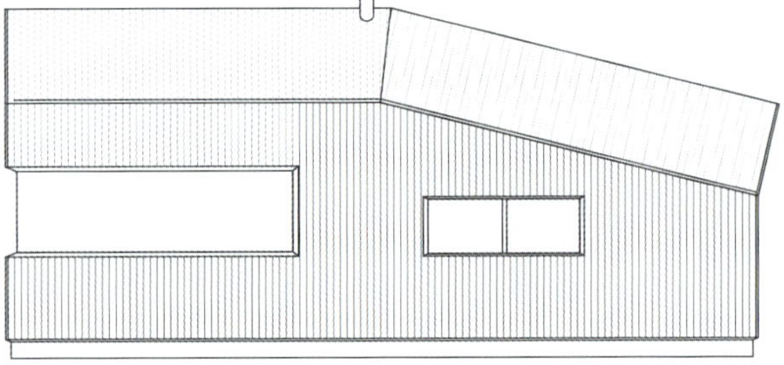

South elevation

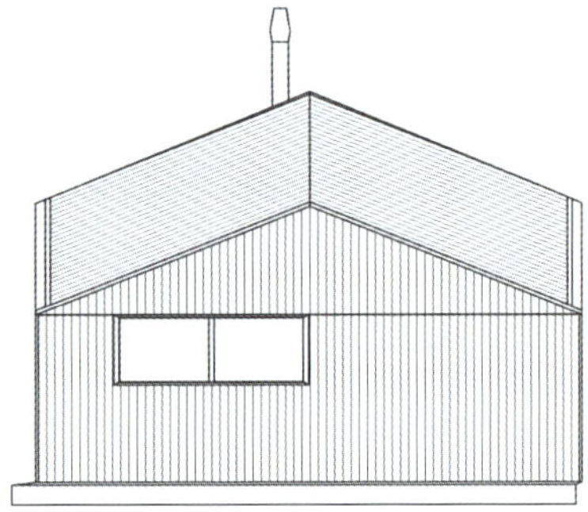

East elevation

VEILING 83 LEIDEN

Mountain

Perched precariously on steep slopes, these contemporary structures offer warmth and security from the often wild weather for climbers, skiers, and adventurers alike, providing an opportunity to live life on the edge.

Bohinj Lake, Triglav National Park, Slovenia

A winning shelter

DublDom Kandalaksha was created and installed as a gift for the town of Kandalaksha, where it will be used as a shelter for tourists and outdoor enthusiasts in both winter and summer. The project is based on the standard modules of DublDom but were fully redesigned for use in the mountains, with the associated low temperatures and high wind loads.

The vibrant red cabin is set in a remote location, and was airlifted in via a helicopter. It appears to float above the ground on a metal frame which rests on six pillars set into the stony terrain. The interior space is designed to cater for up to eight people, with detachable beds (including underneath storage) set around the perimeter. The hall can be used for storing and drying gear and equipment. The interior has a muted color spectrum to avoid competing with the spectacular view from the window.

The large panoramic window is deliberately oriented to the south, showcasing the spectacular views of the Kandalaksha gulf and islands. The sun fills the inner space of the cabin with light and warmth, thus passively heats the house. The cabin is designed for the highest standards of durability and energy efficiency.

DUBLDOM KANDALAKSHA (2018), Kandalaksha, Russia

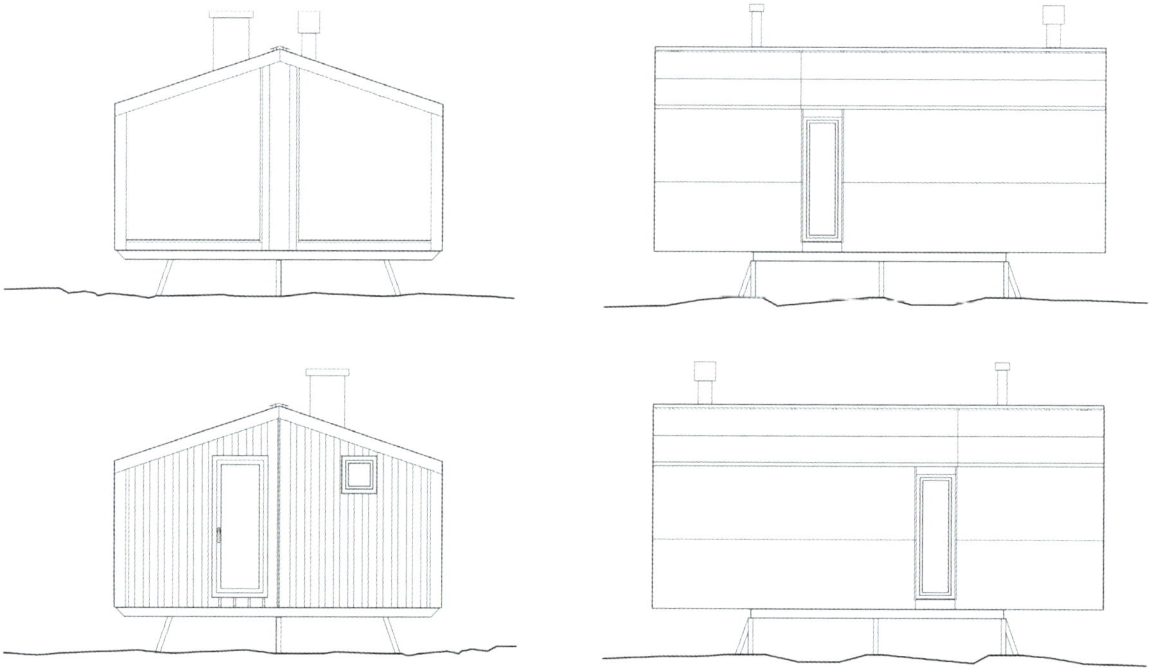

Elevations

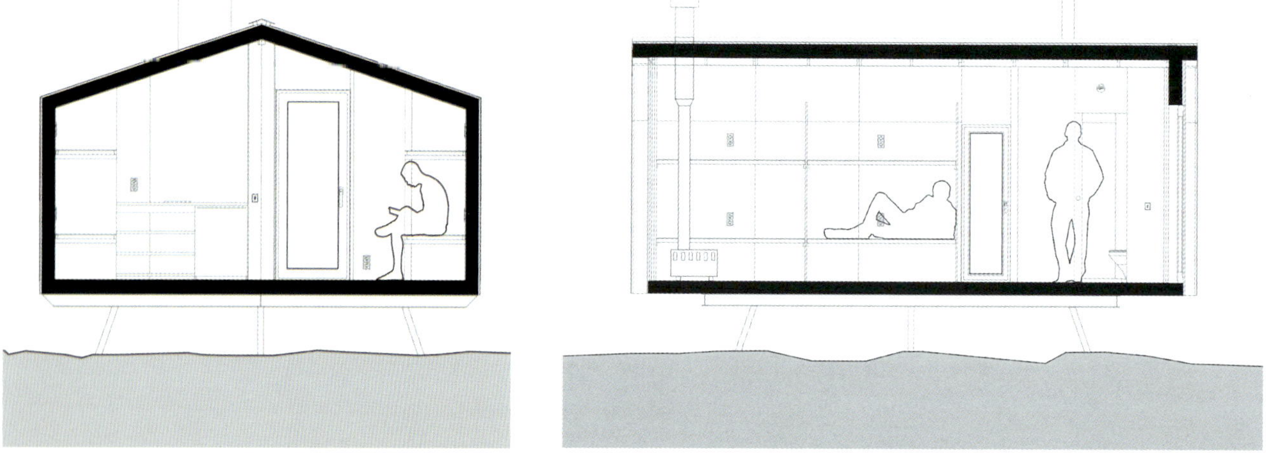

Sections

Traditional meets modern

OPA Form architects have infused new life into this old and neglected barn by adding a modern module that provides all the comfort you might need for a good night's sleep. Situated near the ski resort of Myrkdalen, this revamped traditional building can accommodate a family of four, or a couple on their honeymoon, or a group of ski bunnies.

Seen from the outside there are only small signs of the small barn's transformation. Upon entering, you'll find yourself in the authentic original stable, with its rough surfaces and rustic feel. Here, where the cows were once housed, nothing has changed, but across the room is the new addition: a module clad in bright aspen with a circular entrance.

The modern module is built with the utmost precision and respect for the history of the barn. The addition is self-sufficient, carefully fitted around the existing structure. Part of the module stretches up in between the low beams, resulting in a spacious vertical room where visitors are able to stand upright. The rest of the interior is carefully designed to offer a comfortable sitting and sleeping space during the stay, organized around the central fireplace and the adjacent spacious window. A sculpturesque window stretches out of the old cladding, providing an unparalleled view.

A BARN (2016), Myrkdalen, Norway

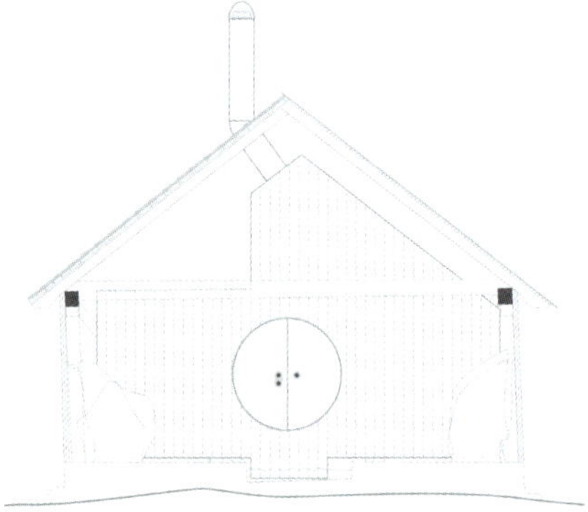

North elevation

South elevation

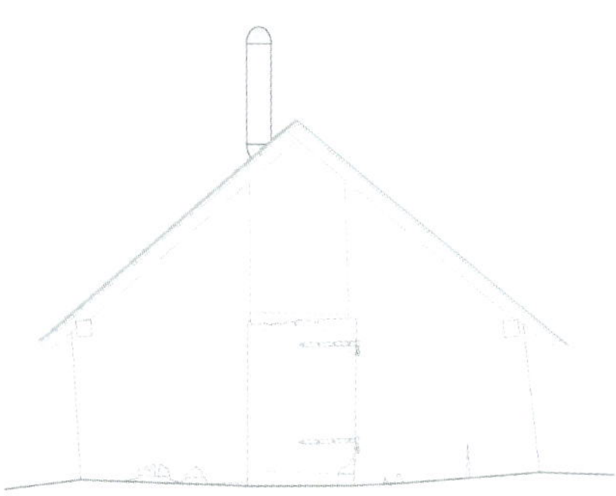

Section A

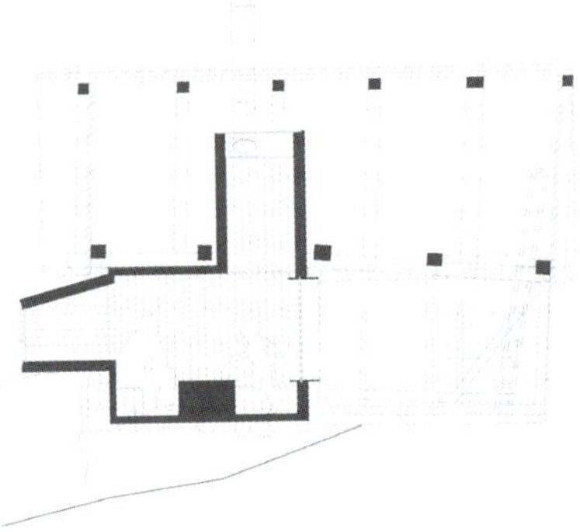

Section B

Blending in

The original Bivak II na Jezerih was first built in 1936 by local alpine climbers. However, its wooden construction finally deteriorated to the point of collapse, and it was airlifted off the mountainside, and donated to the Slovenian Mountaineering Museum.

Its second incarnation was designed using the original bell-shape, to retain the traditional outline. Given its remote location, the aluminum structure was airlifted in via helicopter. Small in scale, the hut is designed to blend into the surrounding limestone rocks. Restrictions on the design process were set by the policies of the Triglav National Park, and the extreme mountain weather and conditions of the site's location.

The hut was built to withstand strong winds, tough alpine conditions, and be easy to maintain given its remote location. It also provides shelter for up to six people, with a cozy atmosphere. Priority during design was given to function rather than attractiveness. Every inch of the shelter is designed for utility, including the durable, non-slippery floor which can withstand crampons, in an emergency. The entrance allows space for drying equipment, with an opening for drainage, and is separate to the small sleeping quarters. But it is the window (which can be boarded up in inclement weather), which affords the greatest prize: the view out onto the surrounding mountains of the national park.

ALPINE SHELTER "BIVAK II NA JEZERIH" (2016), Triglav National Park, Slovenia

Concept

Taking in the view

Perched incongruously on a rocky outcrop below Skuta Mountain, this cabin was designed by Harvard University architecture students in collaboration with the Slovenian architecture studio OFIS, and will serve as a shelter for climbers. Inspired by traditional alpine architecture, this cabin has a pitched-roof and glazed gables, offering views of the Kamnik Alps. The cabin was designed to withstand extreme environmental forces. The windows are triple-glazed to withstand the strong winds and snow loads, and the cabin itself is clad in glass fiber and concrete paneling.

The design consists of three modules, in part to allow for transport and also to divide the space. In order to minimize any disturbance to the site, the modules are fastened onto strategically placed metal pins, which also act as the foundation and strongly anchor the shelter. The first module is dedicated to the entrance, storage, and a small space for the preparation of food. The second one provides space for both sleeping and socializing, while the third features a sleeping area with bunks. Windows at both ends offer beautiful panoramic views of the valley and Skuta Mountain.

ALPINE SHELTER SKUTA (2016), Skuta Mountain, Slovenia

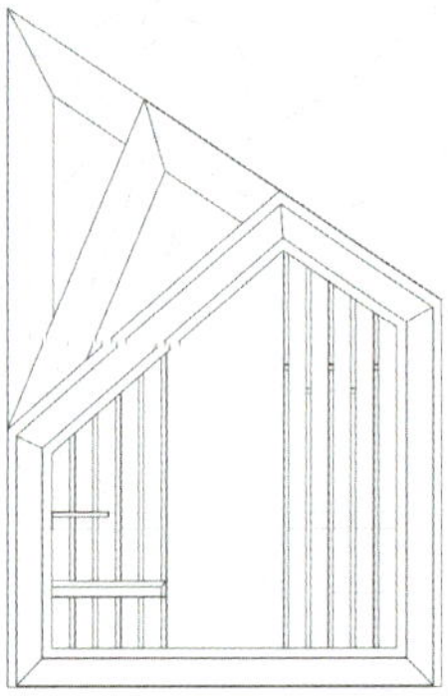

South elevation

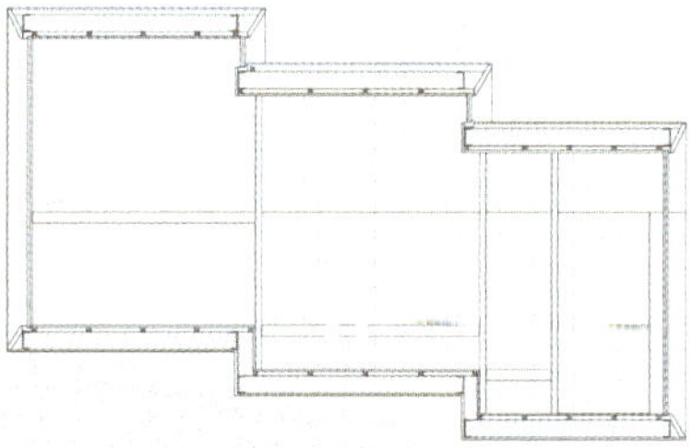

West elevation

Extreme shelter

This spectacular cabin and site enjoys 360-degree views over Slovenia and Italy, with stunning views to Triglav, Soca Valley, and the Adriatic Sea. The rugged terrain is full of caves and abysses, making the site accessible only to hikers, climbers, cavers, mountaineers, and via helicopter to nature lovers and romantics alike.

This self-contained wooden shell is designed to resist the extremely challenging conditions on top of the mountain. Snow cover lasts more than half the year, and the region is known for its ferocious rainstorms and winds, earthquakes, and landslides, so the structural design maximizes shelter stability with a minimal impact on the ground.

The cabin is a compact wooden volume organized with three floor resting platforms. These platforms hang toward the valley and a large glazed panoramic window offers astonishing views. The structure cantilevers over the edge of the mountain, and is held in place by cables. The resting part of the cabin comprises the smallest footprint on the rock. The interior design dictates modesty, subordinate to the function, providing accommodation for up to nine mountaineers.

KANIN WINTER CABIN (2016), Mount Kanin, Slovenia

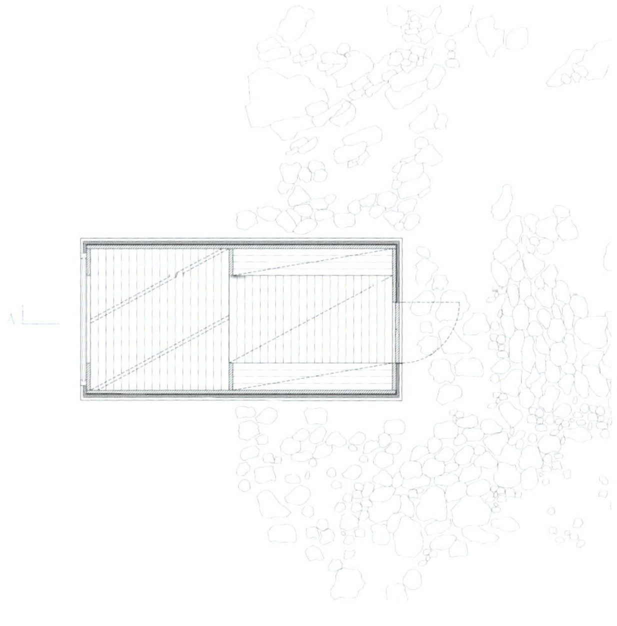

Floor plan

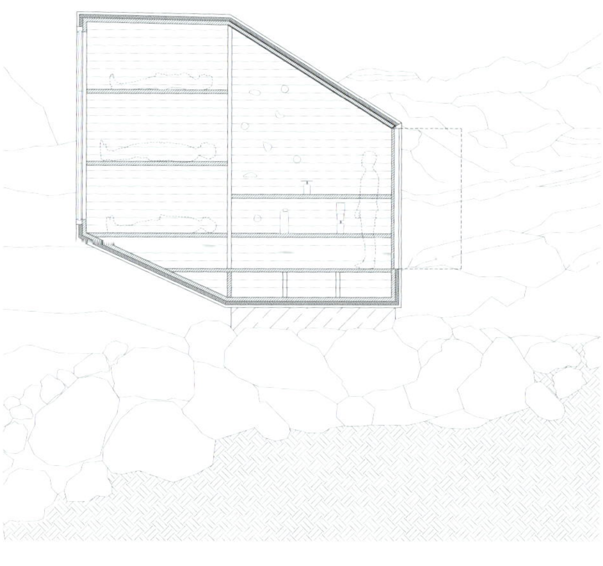

Section

Snowboarders' retreat

This small-scaled weekend retreat for a family of snowboarders sits snugly on a steeply sloping rock bluff in a quiet residential area north of Whistler village. Banking into the rock the cabin is entered from the lowest level, which contains a gear drying room, winter and summer equipment storage, a washroom, and laundry. The living area and kitchen backs into the hill, and a fully glazed facade provides unobstructed views to the mountains across the valley over Green Lake. A bedroom, bunk room, and guest room/den are on the top floor with expansive outward views east; this floor also accesses a private terrace nestled into the rock bluff behind the cabin.

The structure consists of an internally exposed frame of Douglas fir rough-sawn lumber with solid strip structural decking, which sits on the concrete base anchored into the bedrock. The lumber joinery has been designed and engineered to utilize a simple repeated lapped joint at the floor and roof connections. The lap is reversed outward to allow for window dormers at the stair, bunk room, and kitchen. The cabin materials are locally harvested and quarried, including the exterior's red cedar shingles (selected to weather to the tone of the surrounding rock) and the interior cabinetry is designer-built in warm plywood tones and paired with countertops fabricated from local marble.

WHISTLER CABIN (2016). Whistler, British Columbia, Canada

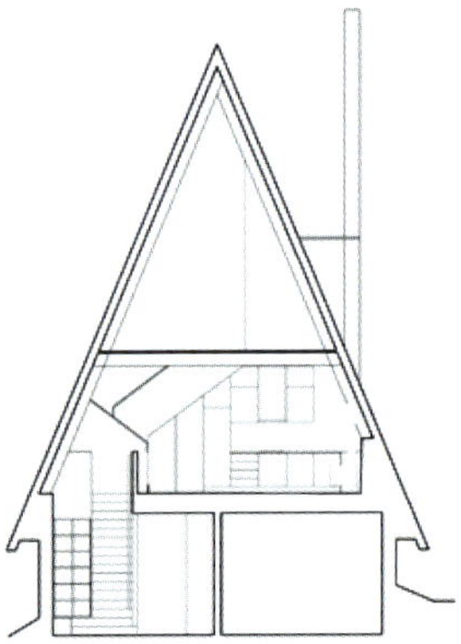

Section

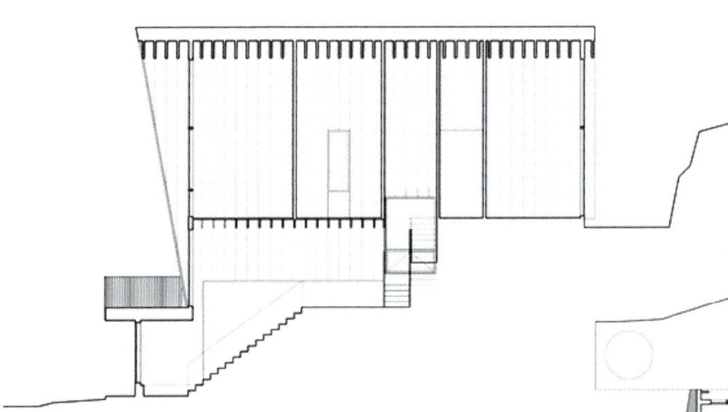

Section

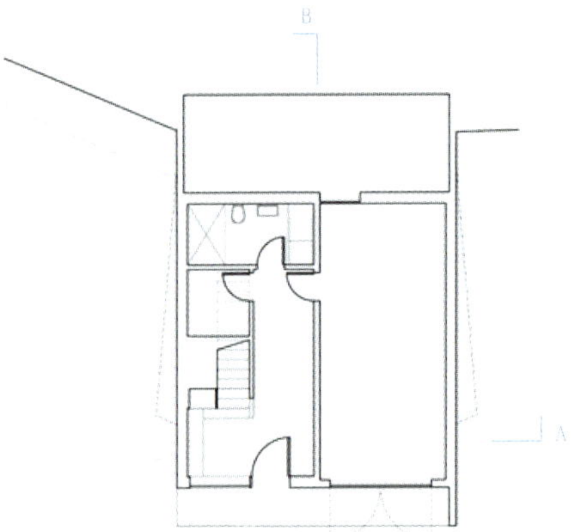

Ground-floor plan

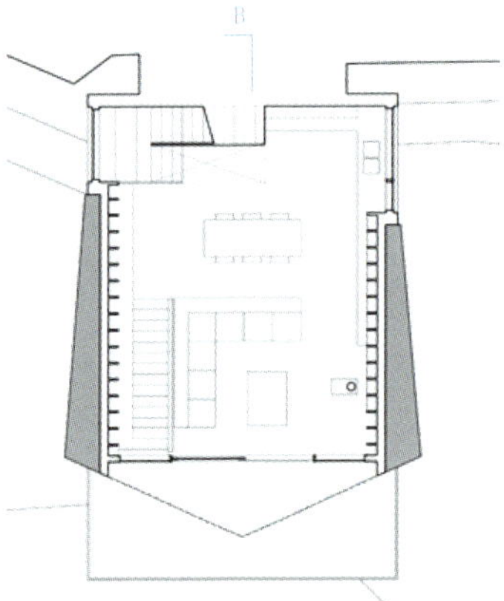

First-floor plan

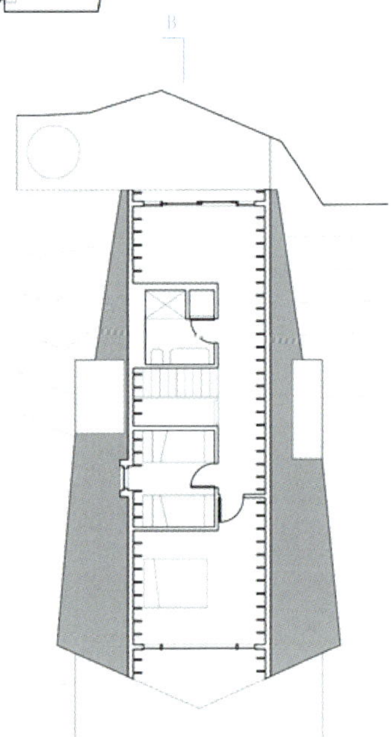

Second-floor plan

Minimum existence

Sitting precariously on a boulder-strewn mountain slope in the Swiss Alps, this alpine shelter contains the very basic architectural elements: a fireplace, a small bed, a fold-down table, and a small window. The small but perfectly detailed wooden cabin, big enough for one person, was a commission by the artist residency Verbier 3d Foundation. It was self-built in the village and transported to its high-altitude placement.

The cabin is hidden inside a projected concrete rock, successfully camouflaged in its surroundings, and referencing the Swiss tradition of hidden bunkers within the mountains. The project integrates the highly urbanized landscape of the Alps and was inspired by the Swiss long-standing tradition of observing the Alps, living with them, hiding inside them.

The architects christened the structure Antoine, after the main character in a novel by Charles-Ferdinand Ramuz, one of the most important Swiss writers. *Deborence* describes a massive rock fall that covered the valley of Lizerne in 1714. Antoine, the main character, survives seven weeks under the rocks before he manages to reach his village, and life. The cabin is a tribute to the alpine experience and to the writer.

ANTOINE (2014), Verbier, Switzerland

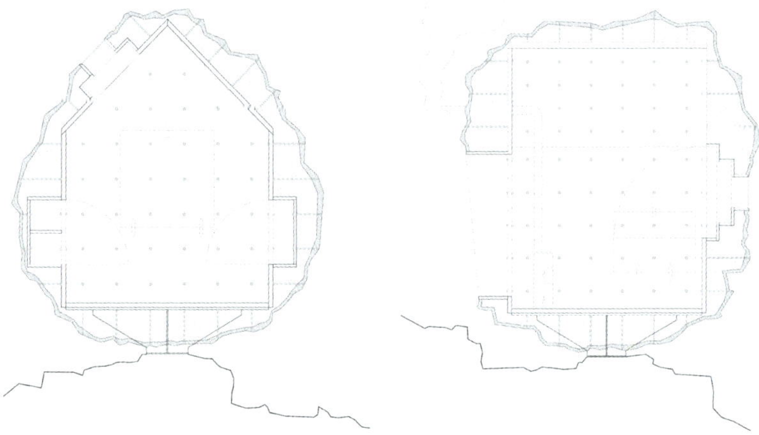

Sections

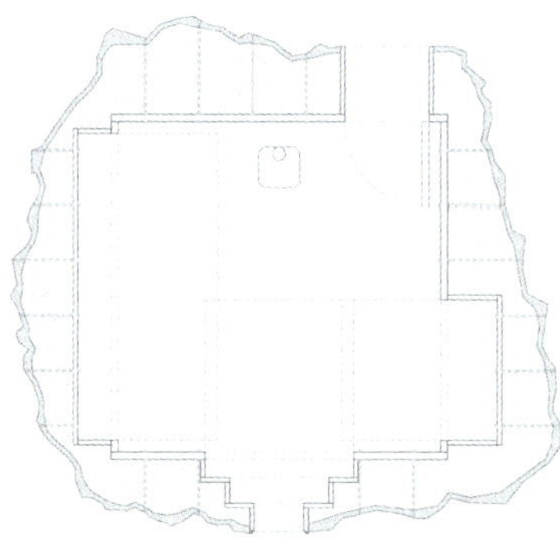

Plan

Sunrise, Joshua Tree National Park, United States

Remote

Set far away from the frantic pace of the modern world, these shelters encourage thoughtful solitude and offer the perfect setting for a technological detox with the chance to truly appreciate the night sky.

Into the wild

Resembling a shipping container, the Ark-Shelter is a purpose-built contemporary retreat to provide the perfect setting for a technology detox. Multiple windows keep the visual focus on the surrounding nature. Large sliding walls at the front can be opened to let the outdoors inside. The milk-glass window in the bathroom gives all-natural incoming light while retaining privacy. An extra module with a glazed ceiling is set on the roof allowing you to sleep under a sky full of stars. The structure, with its low-tech outlook facade, is designed so that it attempts to blend with nature. The spruce timber-wrapped interiors provide a feeling of warmth and comfort.

The pre-fabricated Ark-Shelter is completely off-grid through the use of solar panels, batteries, and rainwater collection. An automated system allows the heating, cooling, and shades to be pre-programmed. The double bed can be raised automatically into the ceiling, revealing a Jacuzzi below. This unexpected addition reveals that the designers have been successful in creating a place that has it all in the least possible space, but with all the possible luxury.

ARK-SHELTER (2018), Kysuce, Slovakia

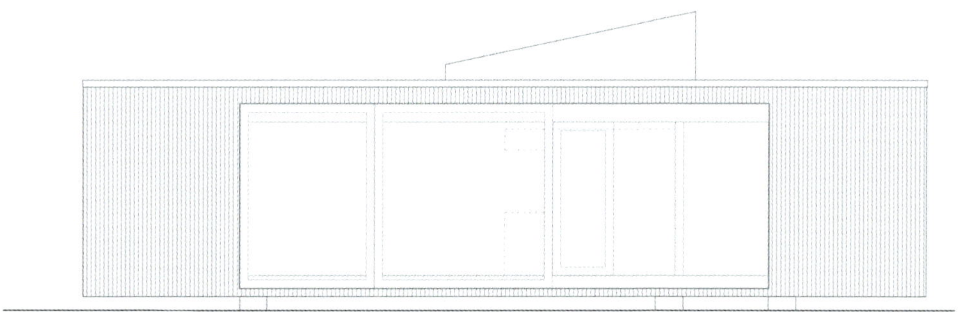

Elevation

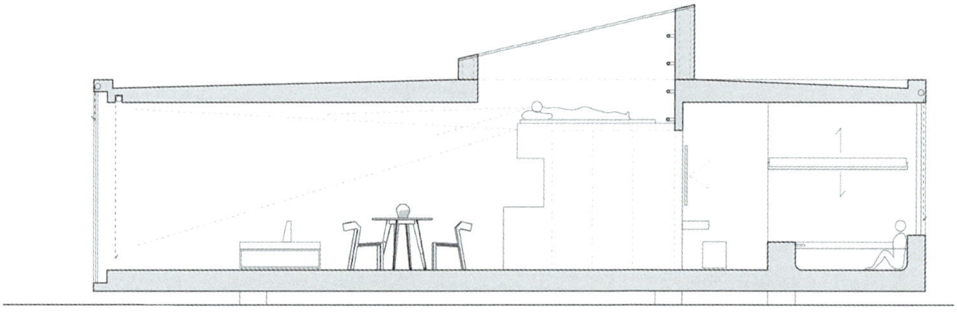

Section

Pitched to perfection

In the middle of the Joshua Tree National Park stand two cabin prototypes with their exteriors naturally weathered to a tawny finish. Within these simple gabled forms lies a complex network that enables them to operate entirely off the grid. Upon arrival, the Folly sets the tone to disconnect from the norm, the expected, and provokes you to connect with the surroundings.

The two structures, designed by Malek Alqadi of Cohesion Studio, are located on the site of an abandoned homestead. The original building's slab was salvaged while raising the original roofline to accommodate a living/dining area and kitchen, a sleeping loft, and a bathroom and wet room. The pitched roof does more than increase livable space; it enables hot air to vent through solar-powered skylights. Locally salvaged steel wraps both buildings, creating a cohesive and naturally weathered appearance. A patio joins the two volumes and includes a sunken outdoor bath. Within the larger volume is a dining area and kitchen, as well as a bathroom. The sleeping area is located in a loft, complete with a skylight for incredible night views. The smaller unit stores equipment on the ground floor, while the open air port, known as the stargazing suite, proves to be the main attraction. The Folly succeeds in providing off-grid living with a measure of luxury without compromising the surrounding environment or guest expectations.

FOLLY (2018), Joshua Tree, United States

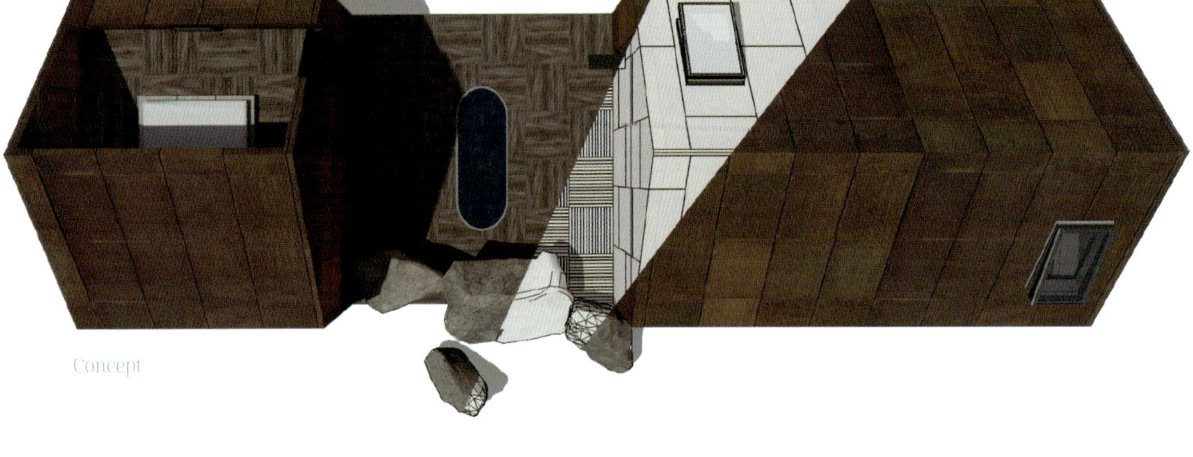

Concept

Legendary accommodation

Located at Castell y Bere, Wales, this unique and angular cabin is known as Arthur's Cave, a nod to the legend of King Arthur seeking refuge in a cave in Wales. But this cleverly designed shelter is very far from being cold, dark, or damp.

Taking its inspiration from the ancient landscape of Wales, the designers used modern construction techniques and sourced local materials wherever possible. The harsh exterior reflects the surrounding stony monoliths and rocky hillsides while the large glass front mirrors the entrance of a cave, and draws you in, through the sitting area, past the small bathroom and into the sleeping den. The structure is a combination of CNC-cut birch plywood ribs and sheathing panels, which act together to form a composite structure.

The exterior is clad in locally sourced larch boards stained black, and the structure is insulated with sheep's wool. The ribbed birch plywood evokes the undulating Welsh hills, as well as the walls of a cave, inviting you to proceed deeper within. The plywood provides both structure, finish, fixtures and fittings—including a plywood sink and bath. The cozy cabin is heated via a small log burner, has hot and cold water, LED lighting, and a self-composting toilet. The interiors are furnished simply, but are stylishly modern.

ARTHUR'S CAVE (2017), Castell y Bere, Wales, United Kingdom

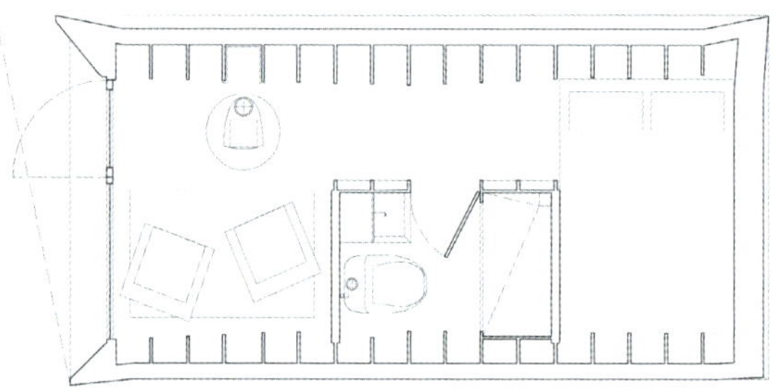

Floor plan

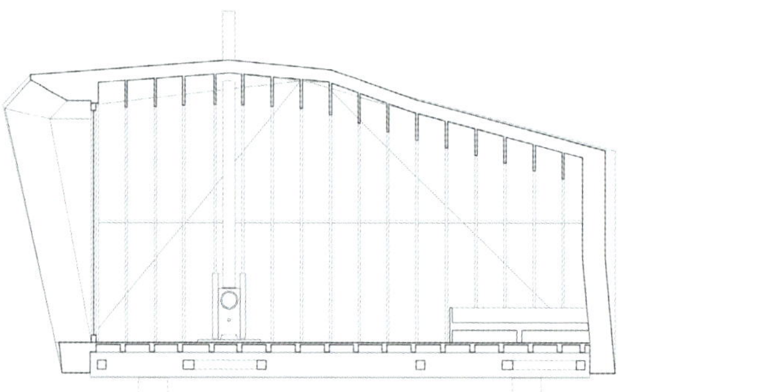

Long section

Beneath the wings of condors

The remote and difficult-to-access Valley of the Condors, known for the birds which soar high above, is so large that there are still unchartered areas, drawing climbers keen to explore. The challenge was to support these outdoor activity enthusiasts by building a shelter for all seasons, while also respecting the terrain. The resulting shelter, made from salvaged materials, is rustic, but provides the basic necessities to exist in this barren landscape: protection from the harsh elements.

This shelter was built by the very volunteers who hike or climb in the region, using reclaimed material from a deteriorated hut, which was transported across 6 miles (10 kilometers). The hut is constructed from recycled corrugated metal, wood, and rocks. The foundation of the structure consists of a base of rocks, with a rough seating arrangement constructed in the level beneath the wooden floor. The main level has basic storage, with a sheet of wood for a prep or sleeping area.

The roof and the north wall are covered with recycled corrugated metal sheets, and placed at a steep angle to prevent accumulation of snow load. The design also took into consideration the constant blowing of the wind, and the salvaged wood was given a coating to protect the structure so that it is able to withstand the stark conditions.

SHELTER FOR THE WANDERER (2016), Valley of the Condors, Chile

East elevation

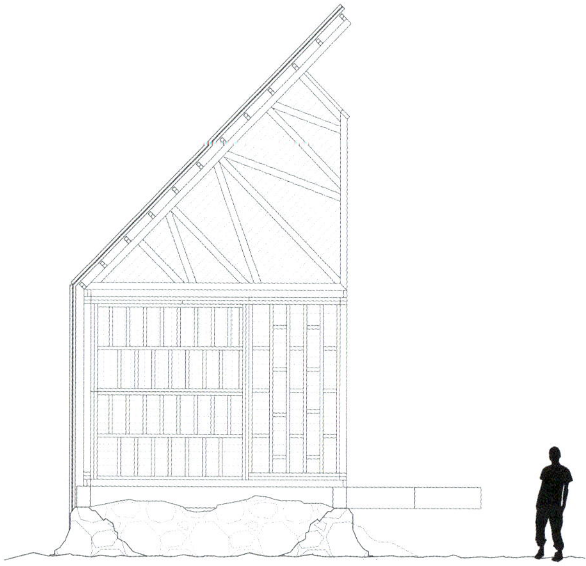

North elevation

Danish deluxe

Taking design to a new level of detail, the Danish design company Vipp has created a steel-and-glass dwelling, filled with their own homeware products, and located in a peaceful hideaway in the Swedish forest. This shelter forms part of the Vipp hotel, one which offers unique rooms at various destinations.

There is no evident link between a pedal-controlled metal wastebin (invented by Vipp 80 years ago) and a shelter but enter the cabin and the philosophy of one long-lasting, functional tool per category is embodied in every item. The starting point of the Vipp shelter is going back to basics; back to nature in a sleek, compact space wrapped in the Vipp DNA. The prefabricated cabin consists of a metal-and-glass rectangular box, set above the ground on stumps, and with two chambers protruding from the roof. One chamber contains a light-well, and the other hosts the bedroom, accessed by a ladder, with a glazed roof allowing you to star gaze at night. The simple steel grid structurally supports the two-level space, where only the bathroom and bed loft are shielded from the main living space.

The landscape is purposely framed by the floor-to-ceiling glass sliding doors on the main level, turning it into the predominant element of the interior space. The dark tones of the interior were carefully selected in order to keep focus on nature. The result is a modern escape, powerful in its simplicity yet packed with exquisitely conceived details.

VIPP SHELTER (2015), Sweden

vipp

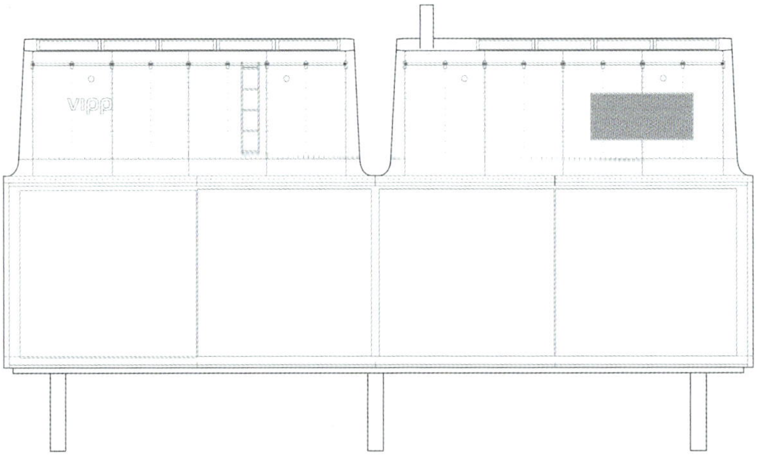

Elevation

vipp

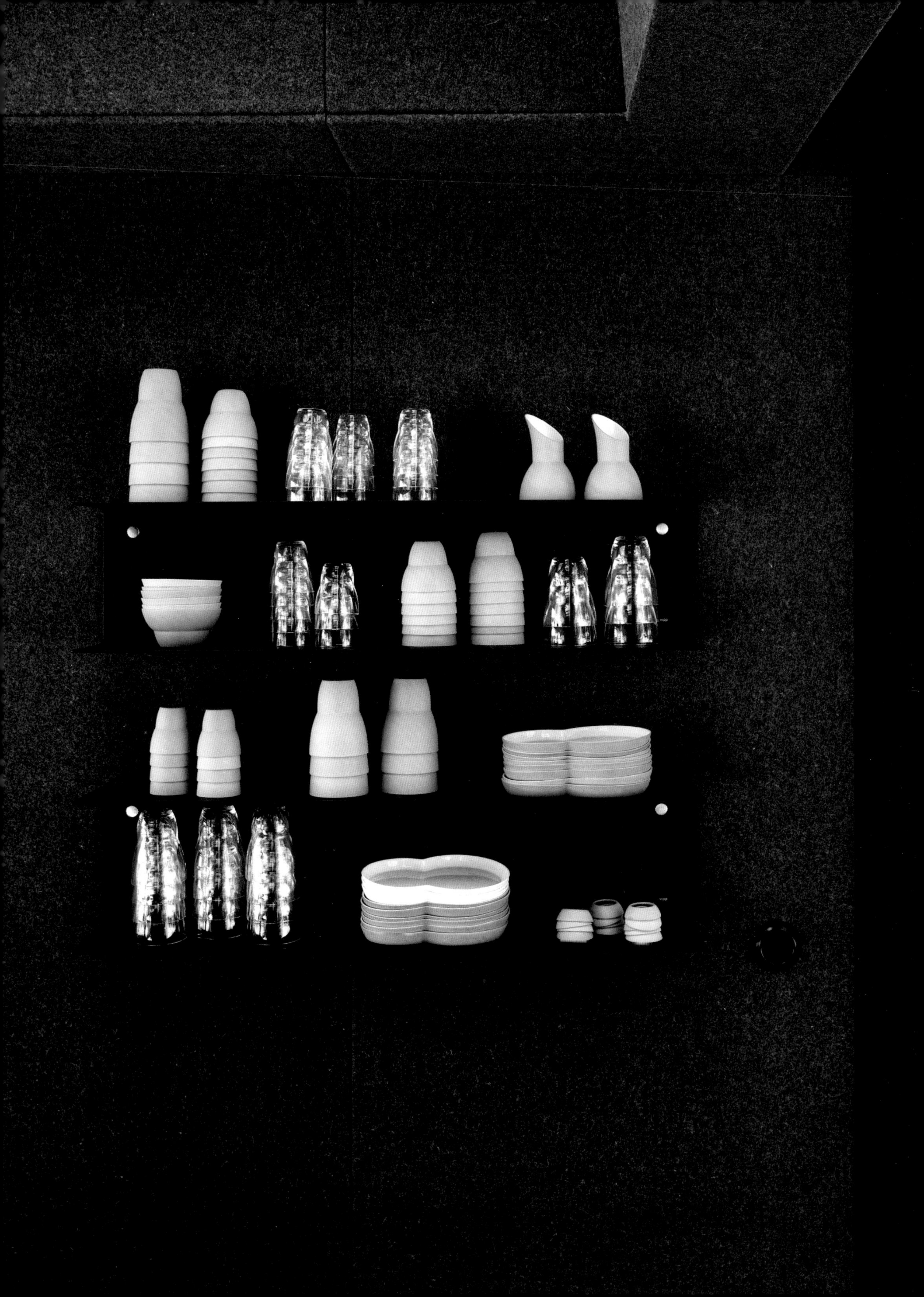

Rural

Enjoy the winning combination of a comforting countryscape and tranquility. Cabins in rural settings allow for a slower pace of life, watching the natural rhythms of the countryside, perhaps accompanied by the distant contented sounds of livestock, or the humming of cicadas.

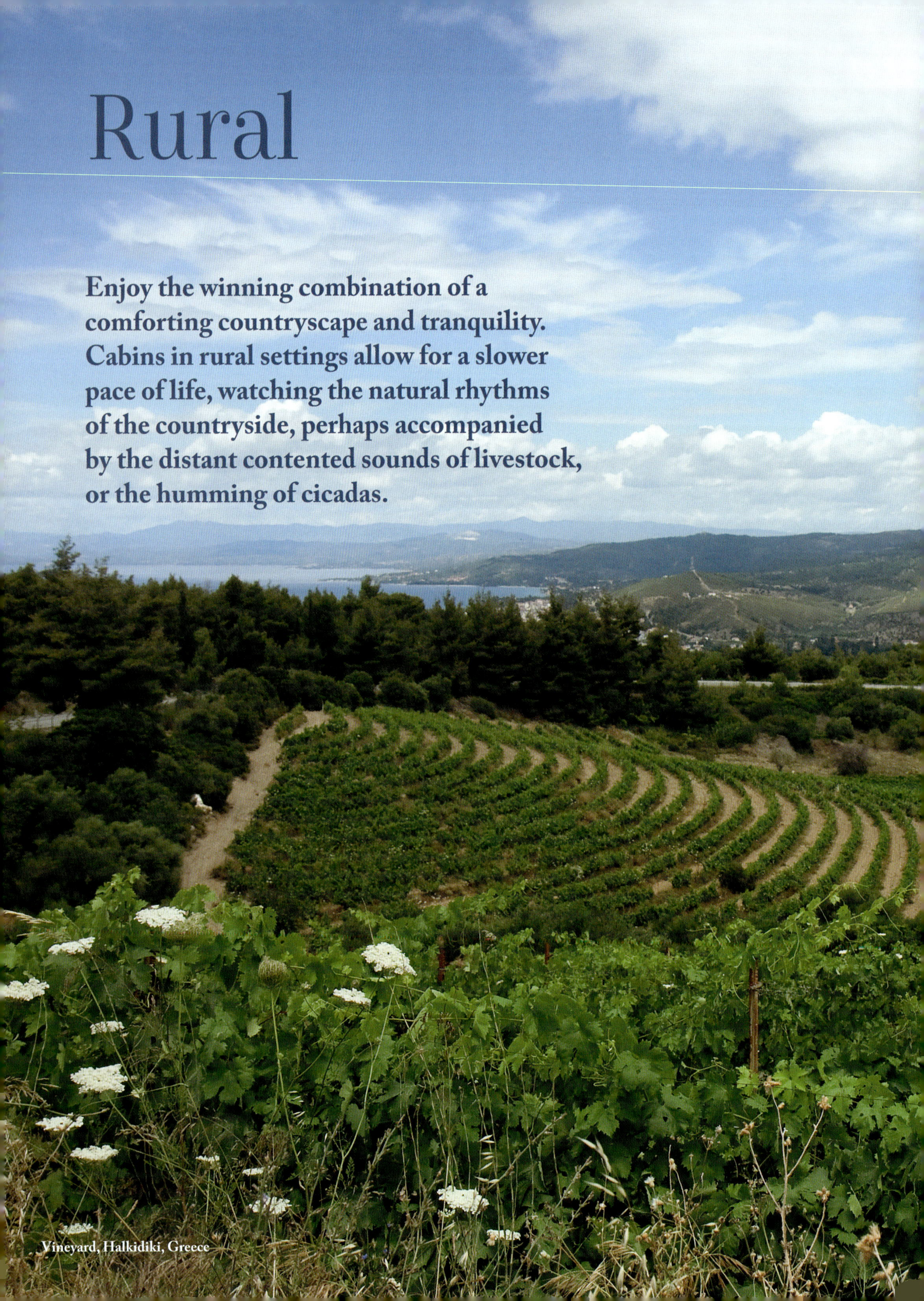

Vineyard, Halkidiki, Greece

Open to the elements

Located in a village on the border between Turkey and Greece, this holiday retreat faces dramatically varying weather conditions. But via a system of pulleys, this building can be manually transformed by its inhabitants, according to the climactic conditions. The no-frills eco-friendly construction sits discreetly in a field of mustard, is powered by solar energy, and collects rainwater for use.

The modestly sized 194-square-foot (18-square-meter) building was prefabricated and transported to its current location by truck. Made from a laminated-timber framework, it is wrapped in stone-wool insulation, with sheets of weatherproofed birch plywood cladding the exterior. The interior is simple, and comprises a kitchen and lounge area, overlooked by elevated beds. A compact bathroom is situated at one end of the dwelling. The horizontal windows allow daylight in when the panels are closed in inclement weather.

When the weather is fine, the panels are raised via the pulleys to allow greater views, and ventilation. A small timber drawbridge-style door transforms into a deck and extends the space in finer weather while a slatted timber canopy provides shade. When the storms hit, the panels are closed, and the interior becomes like the cabin of a yacht, secure against the torrential onslaught.

CABIN ON THE BORDER (2018), Edirne, Turkey

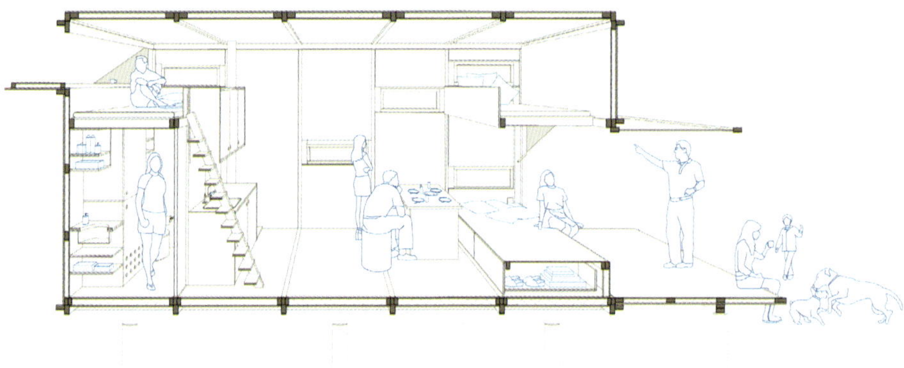

Section

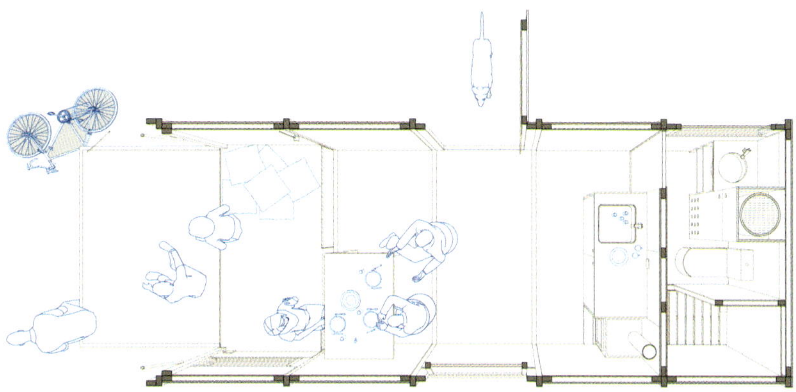

Floor plan

Waste not, want not

This mobile microhome was built for only £20K by Invisible Studio, using salvaged materials and locally grown unseasoned timber. The Trailer is designed to be able to be legally transported on a public highway and used as permanent or temporary accommodation.

The structure is clad in corrugated fiberglass and steel, and internally lined in pre-used shuttering plywood. All of the joinery is from plywood offcuts, including the two ladders. The overhanging corrugated material at each end creates a sheltered porch for external storage.

Inside, the living space runs the length of the Trailer, with a gas stove in the middle. A bathroom and a small kitchen area are set to either side in the widest part of the hexagonal shape. Two sleeping platforms are at either end of the home, accessed by the wooden ladders, and joined by a wooden walkway. High levels of natural light are provided at both gable ends which have interlocking polycarbonate panels. The building is insulated with scavenged insulation, the doors were sourced from a skip, and the skylights were obtained as factory seconds. The project aims to provide a super low cost, versatile, usable space that could act as a kit of parts for any self-builder to improvise around or easily adapt.

TRAILER (2018), Bath, England, United Kingdom

A-framing the view

JR's Hut perches alone on a hill outside Gundagai in rural New South Wales, and stands out like a beacon when the sun's rays reflect off its corrugated iron roof. Eco-friendly and off-the-grid, the building has stunning 360-degree views of the surrounding farmland, the Murrumbidgee River flats, and the Kimo Valley.

The hut's form was inspired by a classic A-frame tent with two open ends, and a corrugated metal roof, to simultaneously provide both refuge from, and connection with, the natural environment. An expressed hardwood structure anchors the building against the wind, defining the interior spaces and framing views of the surrounding undulating hills. Materials needed to be easily sourced and handled on-site by a two-person owner-builder team, and sustainable Australian hardwoods were selected.

The cabin has a stylish simplicity, and its gabled design and use of traditional building material reflects the many farm buildings around the property. The generous use of glass windows is designed to maximize the views. But with a queen-sized bed, floor-to-ceiling windows and an ultra-modern en suite with hot water shower, this comfortable and modern cabin is anything but simple or old-fashioned.

JR'S HUT AT KIMO ESTATE (2017), Gundagai, Australia

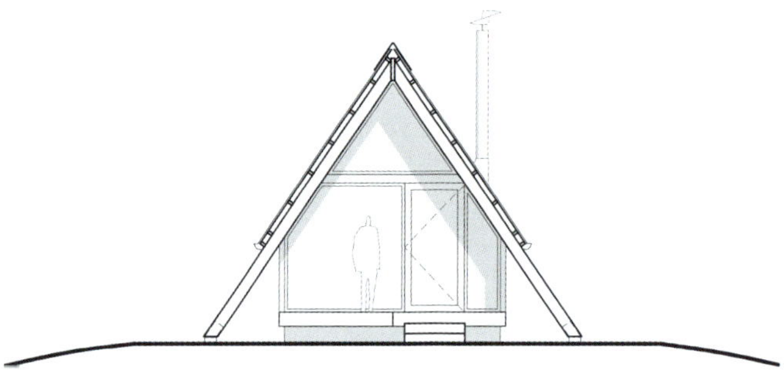

South elevation

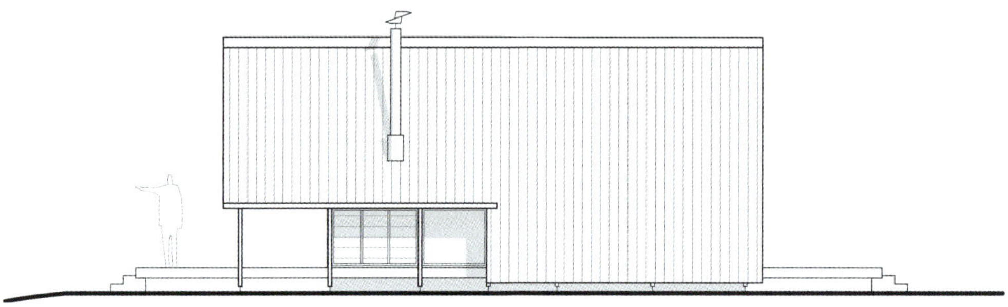

East elevation

BURN ONLY
HARDWOOD

Rising above it all

The Tragata is a modern version of a temporary cabin construction that functions as a short-term residence in western Greece and is used traditionally by farmers and harvesters to look after their crops.

This version is designed to provide a vantage point high above the olive trees, created by lifting the platform up to 16 feet (5 meters) high in order to observe and interact with its surroundings using its 360-degree view. The main structure of the Tragata is a permanent spruce frame construction, covered by detachable panels made out of reeds abundant on the site, and which can be dismounted and stored during wintertime.

The bottom parts of the panels can fold outwards to provide shading during the day, offer natural ventilation, and enable various views of the surroundings. In the same manner, the roof can be folded in half in order to open up and offer views to the night sky. Hidden storage space under the floor allows for mattresses and other belongings to be stored during the day. The result is a eco-friendly place to relax and recharge, while at the same time offering a nod to the historic traditions of its locale.

TRAGATA (2017), Kefalonia, Greece

Section

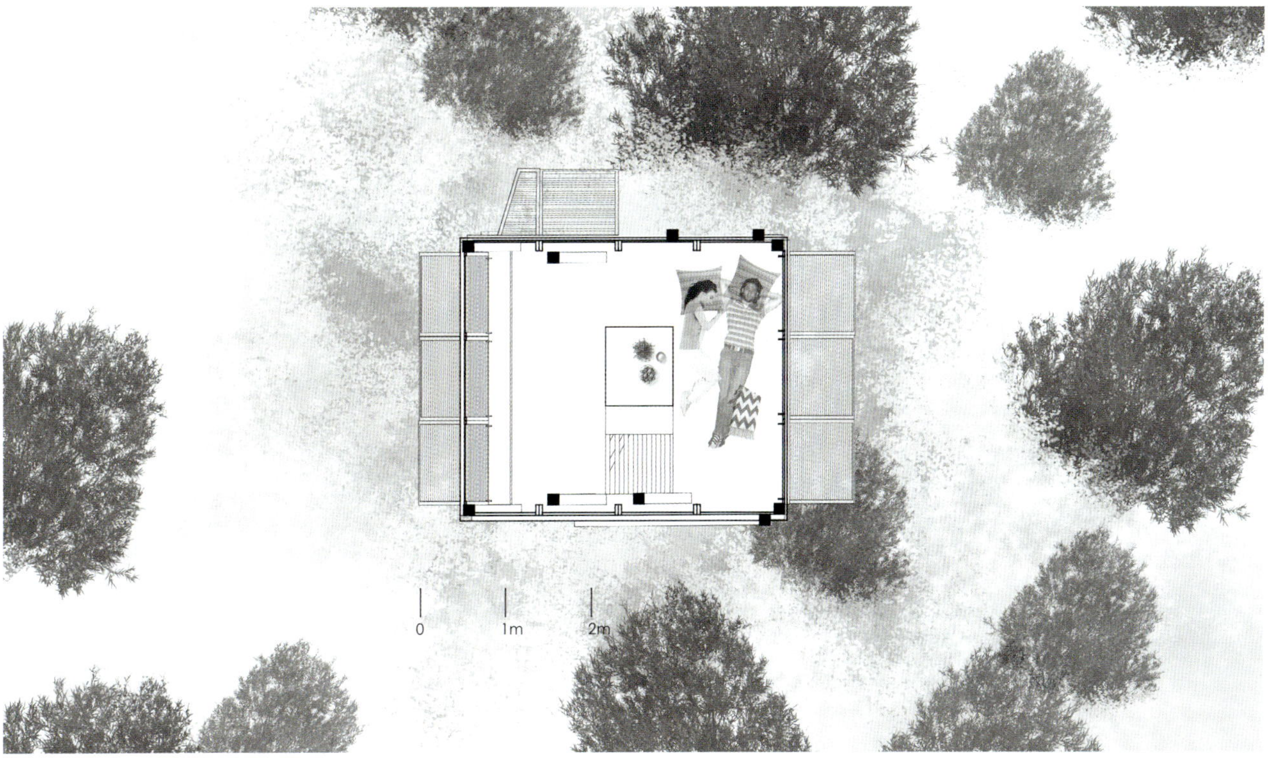

Floor plan

In the grove

Immersed in a pristine olive grove in Halkidiki, Greece, this small summer house is designed to be low maintenance, and in harmony with its surrounds.

Highly experimental in nature, the project employed cutting-edge digital CAD/CAM technology. All of the building components were prefabricated, and put into place with consideration for the position of the sun, to provide shade. The structure can at any time be dismantled, leaving a small footprint on the natural environment. The modest rectangular plan is aligned to the cardinal points and is subdivided into smaller rooms, connected by a corridor aligned with the adjacent olive trees.

The exterior envelope is a lightweight metallic surface which wraps around the structure. Its lightness enables it to be moved, to provide maximum flexibility. The envelope's perforated textile-like pattern is inspired by the shade of the olive trees. As the sun moves during the day the interior spaces are filled with ever-changing shadows, giving each room its own distinct character.

OLIVE TREE HOUSE (2016), Halkidiki, Greece

Fairytale appearance

This magical lakeside cabin, on the edge of woodlands in the village of Nouvelles, Belgium, needed to be lightweight, simple, and economical. The new 376.7-square-foot (35-square-meter) cabin replaced an old dilapidated timber structure and it was important that it would appear as if it could have been there for years and that it had a dialogue with the local vernacular of agricultural buildings.

The result was a rustic wooden structure, featuring an all-black exterior, a steeply pitched roof and a smoking chimney. Both the structure and external cladding are wood, built using trees felled and milled from the surrounding woodland. To create the black facade, the architects mixed wood stain with recycled tractor engine oil. Concrete strip foundations grounded the building to its site. Inside, wooden ceiling beams are left exposed overhead, while walls and floor are lined with oriented strand board (OSB), a type of robust engineered panel made up of wooden strands.

Apart from a wood-burning stove that provides the building's heating, there are no fixed furnishings in the main space. This allows it to accommodate different activities, from working to sleeping or socializing. A toilet and washroom are located at one end, while a small reception area can be found at the other. All three rooms open out to a wooden deck, from which residents can look out over the lake.

WOODLAND CABIN (2015), Nouvelles, Belgium

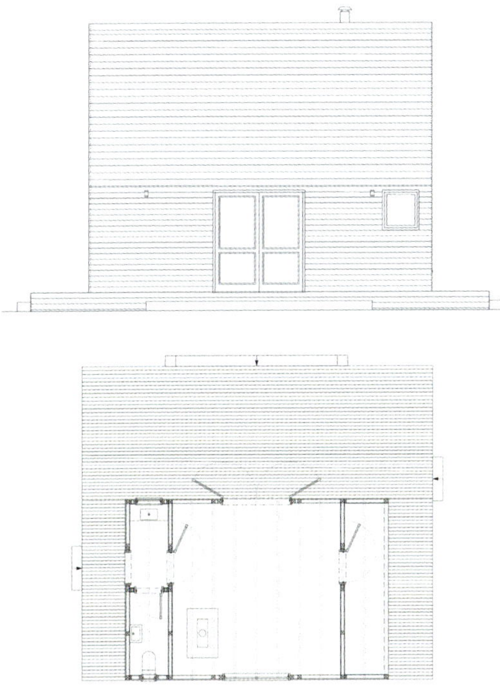

Elevations

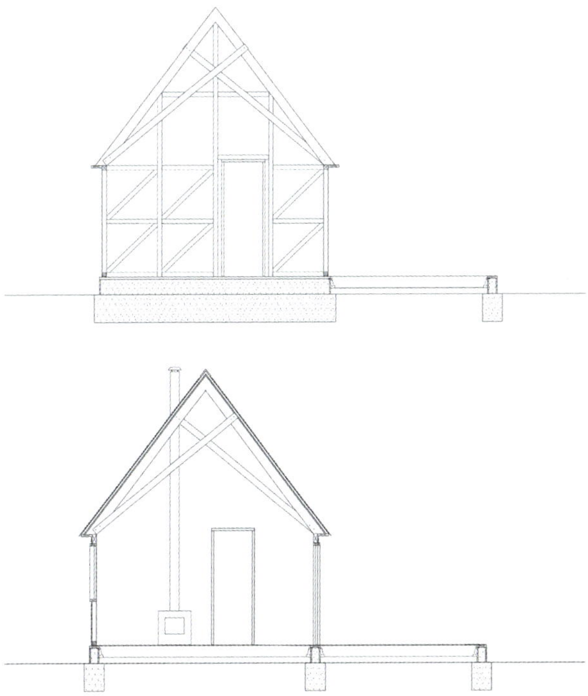

Sections

Normandy coast, Saint-Martin-en-Campagne, France

Water

Watch the ever-changing moods of the water while staying dry in a shelter set beside a lake, a river, or within sight of the ocean, or make a retreat into the cozy comfort of the cabin after a day in the water.

Thinking outside the box

At first sight, the isle of Fleinvær may appear rough and windswept, but it has a vulnerable fragility to it, with spare yet vulnerable vegetation, and nesting sites for gulls and seabirds. The profound respect for the natural surroundings is reflected in the size of the constructions and their careful adaptation to the terrain. The project's modest contact with the ground level also makes removal of the buildings possible, without extensive damage to the natural environment.

The idea was to create a series of small buildings that could adapt to the terrain, instead of having one large imposing structure. The nine buildings consist of four tiny sleeping cabins, one sauna, a bathhouse, a kitchen, a creative room, and a "thinking box." The various parts are linked via a series of footbridges and paths, imposing only a modest interference with the ground. Each building is raised above ground level using light foundations. The facades are clad in leftover materials from the building work.

Initially the Arctic Hideaway was meant as a workplace, and a writing lodge for use by artists, musicians, and other creative souls. This project came to fruition thanks to the efforts of Håvard Lund, a recognized jazz musician in Norway. The small isle offers a secluded working environment in an area of awe-inspiring natural beauty, surrounded on all sides by wild sea, and provides a feeling of complete detachment.

ARCTIC HIDEAWAY (2017), Fleinvær, Norway

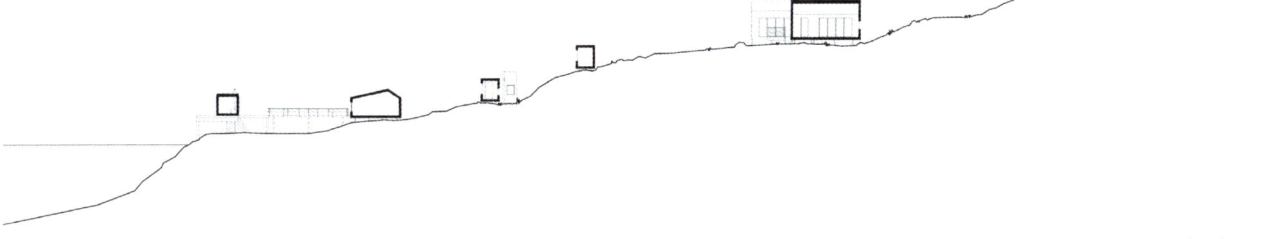

Sections

Site plan

I spy

Since its introduction in Victorian times, the humble British beach hut has become as familiar on seafronts as fish-and-chips. With this in mind, the architects wanted to capture the nostalgia and fondness surrounding these huts with a new physical form that doesn't lose the spirit of the original.

The result is an eye-catching design, which resembles the traditional slot binoculars so often found at the seaside. The new beach hut is responsive to views, light, and the elements, unlike traditional stationary huts. The Spy Glass is built on a recessed turntable so that the picture window of the hut can be turned to view the rising sun over the shimmering sea, or toward the twinkly lights of Eastbourne Pier in the evening, or in any 180-degree direction as desired. The hut will in this way and in a sense react to daily life around it.

The Spy Glass is built from a combination of robust nautical materials and to the same measurements as a traditional beach hut. Inside are a daybed, table and two stools. The timber-clad entrance door has an overhang, with two porthole windows, and there's an external shower for use after a dip in the sea.

THE SPY GLASS (2017), Eastbourne, England, United Kingdom

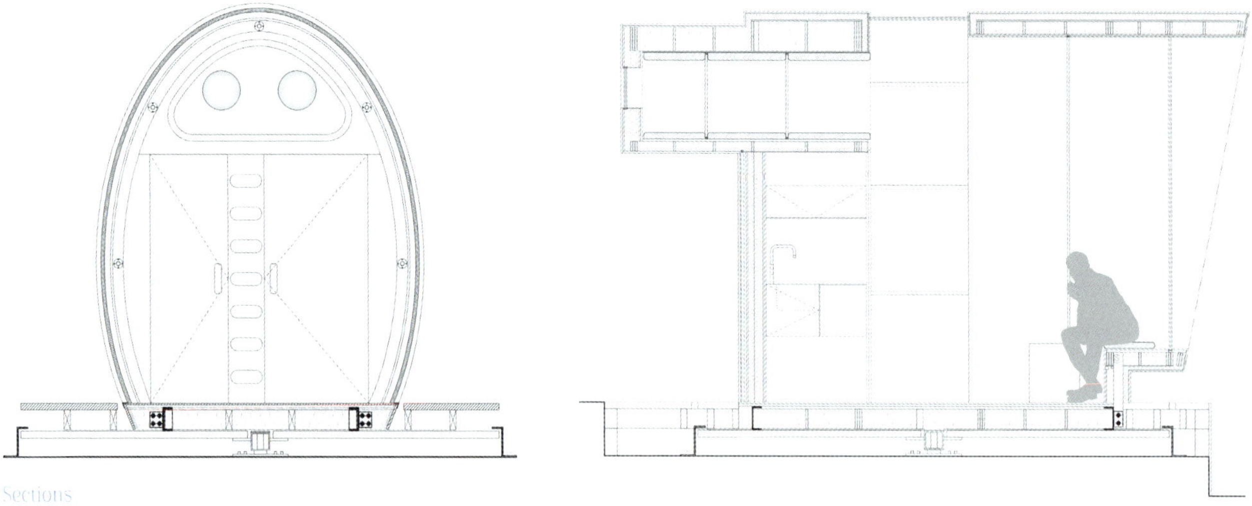

Sections

Outside in

The Outside House, comprising two pavilions, is designed as a place to live outside, using the higher-elevation location on Maui as a cool-temperature retreat for the owner.

The enclosed pavilion is called the Mauka after the Hawaiian word for "inland toward the mountains." Containing a bed and a writing desk, it is oriented to look up the site's lava flow and catch the first light of sunrise. For the remainder of the day, the room is in cool shade for daytime reading or napping. To minimize its impact on the site, the pavilion is raised off the ground on concrete blocks. The outdoor pavilion is named the Makai after the Hawaiian word for "seaward." This pavilion is a prefabricated galvanized steel structure forming a roofed platform that shelters a deck, small outdoor kitchen, and hidden outdoor shower that are all open to views of the Pacific Ocean and the neighboring island of Kaho'olawe.

The center of the Outside House is the ever-changing ground between the pavilions. The unbuilt areas of the Outside House—lichen on the lava, a curved rock wall, an endemic Mamani tree—are the essence of daily living in this place. For greater eco-friendliness, the pavilions are designed to be minimally connected to the ground and to be demountable. The Outside House is intended to demonstrate the client's eco-centric worldview, a perspective that is rooted in the Hawaiian concept of *aloha aina*—love of the land.

OUTSIDE HOUSE (2017), Hawaii, United States

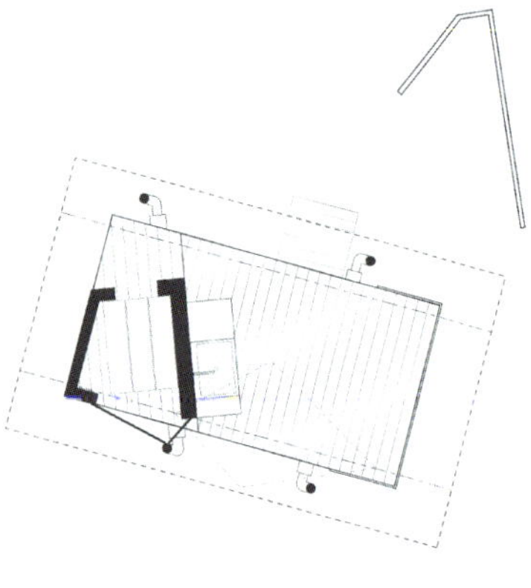

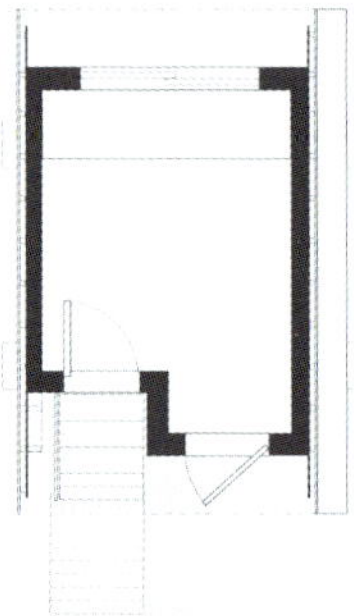

Floor plan

great tide rising

Escaping the hordes

Located on the western coast of France, where fleets of fierce Vikings once landed, this revamped cabin was originally a 1950s concrete fishing shack. Strict French planning regulations meant that the size or shape of the shack could not be altered. Ingenious design, however, ensured that the shack was modernized inside and out. The roof was redone and exterior insulation added by using a light champagne-colored galvanized metal cladding, while two large sliding windows were installed, opening the house to the horizon.

The interior design is minimalistic but cleverly takes advantage of each and every space. There is a loft including the double bed. The main living area, with expansive views to the sea, contains a couch but also a table for eight people and designer folding chairs. At the core of the structure is a white-tiled area where the toilet and a glazed shower mezzanine are sited. The small kitchen faces the main living area, and leads to the large outdoor terrace, which expands the living space to the stunning seaside. The updated and revamped Viking Seaside Summer House rests on a rock, facing the sea and set in a beautiful environment, offering a sense of escape.

VIKING SEASIDE SUMMER HOUSE (2017), Fermanville, France

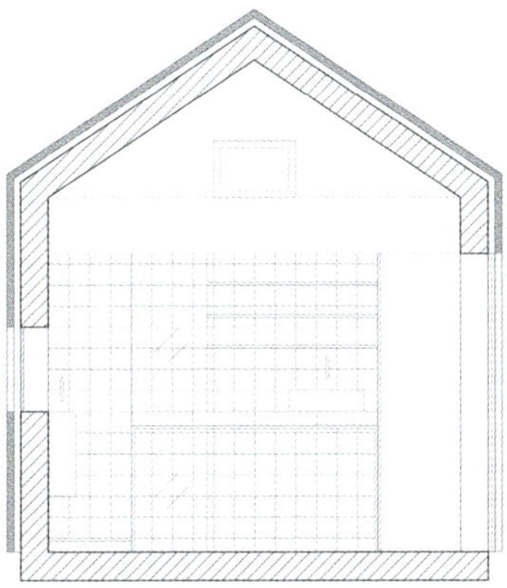

North elevation

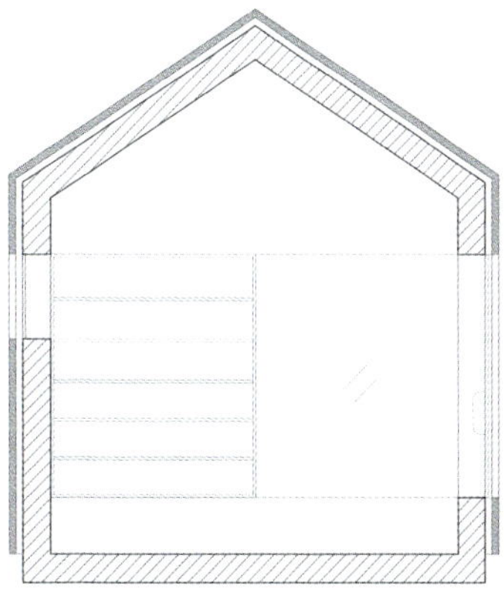

South elevation

LA CALYPSO
LES DAUPHINS ET LA LIBERTÉ
LES REQUINS
A LA RECHERCHE DE L'ATLANTIDE
Métaphysique de mer
NORMANDIE COTENTIN

Water-bourne

DD16 is a modern modular compact cabin designed to be placed in remote places and extreme conditions. The structure consists of two prefabricated DublDom modules, and is robust enough to withstand a Russian winter, but also light enough to float on water. This was successfully demonstrated by installing modular pontoons underneath, and positioning the cabin on a lake.

The frame is made of laminated wood while the exterior is finished with composite aluminum, which is lightweight and resistant to the elements. Polyurethane foam is used as an insulation, making the walls more rigid and which enables lighter finishing materials to be used inside, such as thin plywood.

This off-grid cabin uses solar power for electricity and sources its water from the lake. At just 172 square feet (16 square meters), the internal space makes the most of the structure's size, while retaining a cozy level of comfort. The cabin features a double bed with underneath storage, a full-sized bathroom with an eco-friendly toilet, shower and tub, and a living area with a wood-burning stove. The kitchen is small but functional, and the dining table is attached to the ceiling with a cable, allowing it to be secured to the wall when not in use. Large windows allow natural light to penetrate and also help to increase the sense of space inside. The outdoor deck expands the available space in finer weather, and brings the outdoors inside.

ultralam
ElastoKAM
DOMCLUB

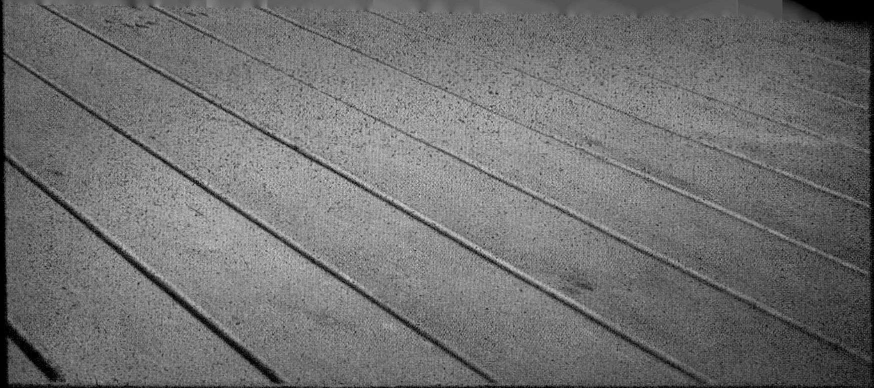

Lakeside retreat

This unique recreational house is situated on a small island in a Dutch lake area, forming a subtle frame that captures the views from the inside out and outside in. The cabin is designed in such a way that it can customize the interaction with the surrounding nature, and its orientation is based on the rising and setting of the sun. One of the glass facades can be completely opened so that the wooden outdoor terrace becomes part of the interior, and the dark wooden facade can be folded open, creating a panoramic view to nature and further blurring the distinction between interior and exterior. By opening this part of the facade the wooden floor of the living area is now directly connected to the water enabling the inhabitants to access the lake from the living room. Despite its petite size, Island House contains all the requirements for comfort, for all sorts of weather. A shower, toilet, kitchen, closets, storage, and other functions are all integrated into a double wall. The fireplace, which hangs from the ceiling, can be rotated toward the outdoor terrace for those cozy summer evenings.

ISLAND HOUSE (2012), Breukelen, the Netherlands

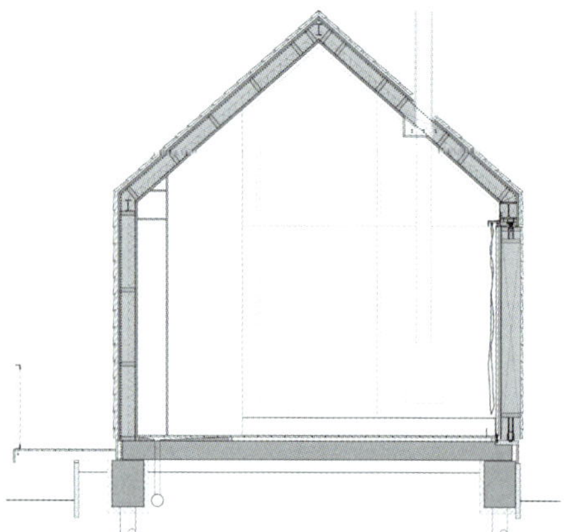

Section

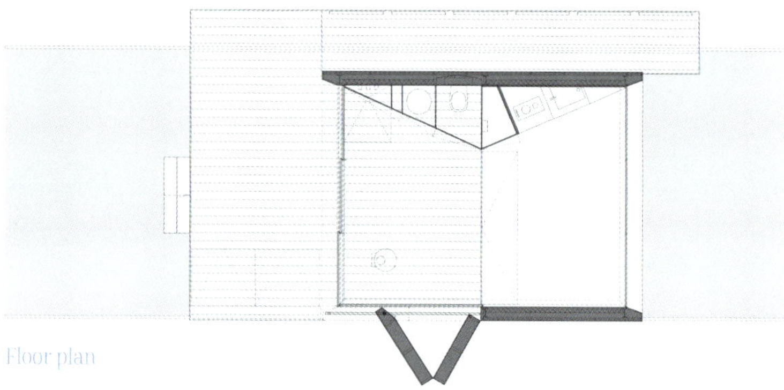

Floor plan

Urban

Cabins make a surprising appearance even in built-up locations, or offer an impressive observation point to view the cityscape. Where you might least expect to find cabins, the lure of escape can still be found.

Amsterdam, the Netherlands

Leave no trace

CABN is an off-grid and self-contained cabin designed to provide a place to get away from everything, and digitally detox. Set in the picturesque Adelaide Hills on typical natural scrubland, this particular CABN (named "Jude") is designed to make as little impact on the environment as possible. Its eco-friendliness extends to employing composting toilets, using rainwater catchment, and solar power. In addition, local sources of material were used wherever possible in order to make the build as sustainable as possible and sympathetic to the environment.

One of the most important elements in the design was to be able to bring the outdoors in, so large windows were installed to create and invite space. The interior has a minimalist look, with the windows providing cross-ventilation. The use of natural timber and Scandinavian aesthetics affords a warm and welcoming environment, and also allows the CABN to blend into or reflect the surrounding native flora.

The interior includes a king-sized bed, an additional king-sized single bed, an indoor shower, and a kitchen. The large windows look out over rolling hills. The CABN is designed to be movable, so it can be relocated to any rural or even a suitable suburban block or other urban environment, as desired. The renewable energy supplies enough to run the small appliances, and the ceiling fan.

CABN "JUDE" (2017), Adelaide, Australia

CABN
Jude

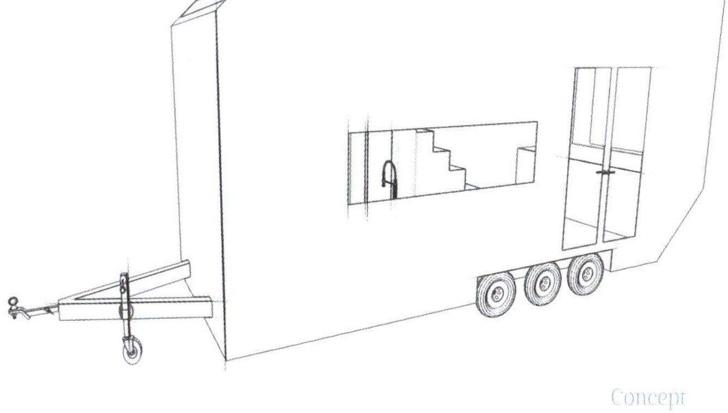

Concept

Sliding walls

The flexible design of Garden House combines a minimal footprint with maximum connection to the natural environment, and allows the user to adapt the layouts according to varying weather conditions.

The core of the house consists of an inner shell of double glass with an overarching steel roof and measures at its core 20 feet by 13 feet (6 meters by 4 meters). But the size can be increased to nearly 50 feet (12 meters) simply by sliding the walls. The structure sits on a lifted platform, with four rails that slide timber- and glass-walls to reveal or enclose the cabin.

When the house is completely closed, it provides a warm and cozy shelter from the elements. When the weather is a little warmer and sunnier the wood protective shell slides open, leaving the glass shell in place, allowing maximum light but still affording protection from the rain and wind. In sunnier weather, the glass shell can be parted to create an outdoor living space. By sliding the glass shells out an enormous indoor space is created. This provides enough space for a 32-foot-long (10-meter-long) table and at least 30 guests. By adapting its shape to changes in its environment, the Garden House is just another organism within the larger ecosystem.

GARDEN HOUSE (2016), Eindhoven, the Netherlands

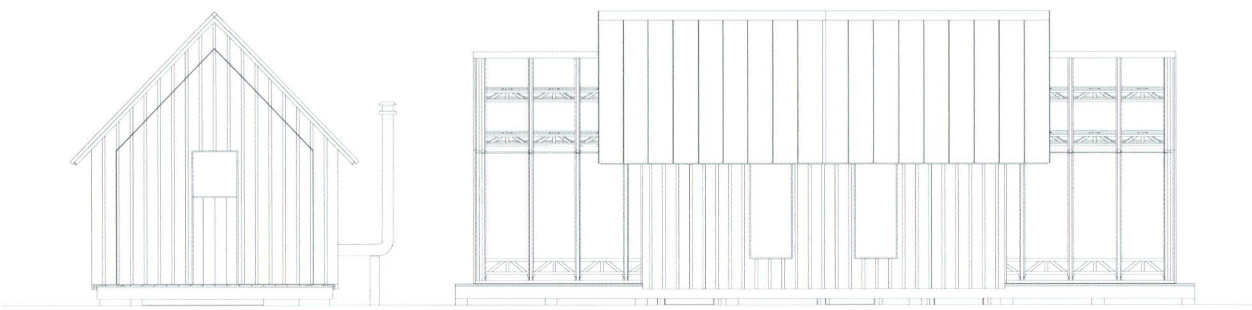

Elevations

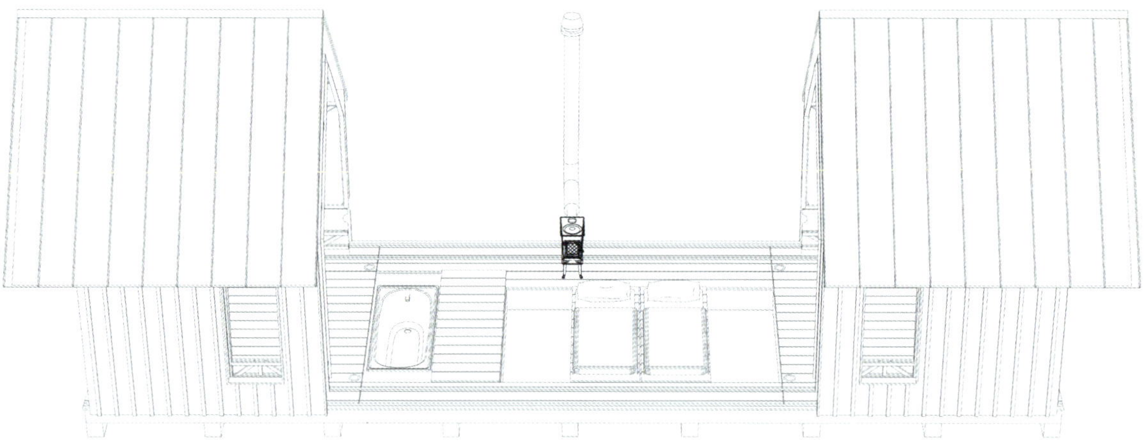

Concept

Print it

The Urban Cabin transforms a former industrial area in Amsterdam from a vast empty space into an urban retreat, complete with pocket park and outdoor bathtub. It is entirely 3D printed with black colored bio-plastic and can be fully recycled and reprinted in the following years. The cabin forms part of research into compact and sustainable dwelling solutions in urban environments.

The cabin comprises a mini-porch and indoor space in which a sofa can be doubled up as a twin bed. Outside there is a 3D-printed bath. This tiny gabled cabin has a window at one end, while the other contains the entrance and porch. The walls are designed with angular protrusions, adding extra structural stability, as well as visual interest.

The design plays with the relations between indoor and outdoor spaces, creating luxury within a minimum footprint. Its external structure showcases different types of facade ornament, form-optimization techniques, and smart solutions for insulation and material consumption. The floor and stepped porch are combined with a concrete finish creating a beautiful pattern that extends into a path in the pocket park.

URBAN CABIN (2016), Amsterdam, the Netherlands

Elevation

Down the rabbit hole

Perched on the edge of a cliff overlooking the city of Bergen, Tubakuba provides an enticing option for explorers young and old, and is readily accessible via public transportation. The primary feature of the structure is the rabbit hole-like entry, made of bent timber scraps which mimic the horn of a tuba, giving it its distinctive name, "Tuba Cube."

This creative project is the result of a design-build workshop at Bergen School of Architecture lead by Espen Folgerø at OPA Form architects, and is available for rent on a nightly basis. It's completely off-grid, but a wood stove provides sufficient heat while the wooden-fiber insulation not only maintains the warmth, but allows the structure to breathe. The interior is Scandinavian minimalist in character yet cozy with built-in plywood furniture, including a loft-style bed.

Made from 95 percent wood, the cabin has four very different external walls. The iconic tunnel consists of curved long strips of pine mounted in layers to provide sufficient strength, while the south wall is clad with untreated larch, which will turn gray with time. The charred larch cladding is made with a traditional Japanese method, which inhibits decay. The wall facing the valley is entirely of glass and affords commanding views of Bergen set below in the valley.

TUBAKUBA MOUNTAIN HUB (2014), Bergen, Norway

Section

PROJECT CREDITS

26–33 **A SHELTER FOR ALL SEASONS**
Casa R | Felipe Lagos Novoa – Architect || tucroquis.com
LOCATION Vilches, Chile
COMPLETED 2018
AREA 1,033 ft² (96 m²)
PHOTOGRAPHY Felipe Lagos Novoa

34–41 **NORDIC DESIGN**
Klein A45 | BIG | Bjarke Ingels Group || big.dk
LOCATION Upstate New York, United States
COMPLETED 2018
AREA 183 ft² (17 m²)
PHOTOGRAPHY Matthew Carbone

42–45 **FEATHERED FACADE**
Birdhut | Studio North || studionorth.ca
LOCATION Windermere, British Columbia, Canada
COMPLETED 2017
AREA 100 ft² (9.3 m²)
PHOTOGRAPHY Studio North

46–55 **A BIRD IN THE NEST**
ORIGIN Tree House | Atelier LAVIT || atelier-lavit.com
LOCATION Château de Raray, France
COMPLETED 2017
AREA 376.7 ft² (35 m²)
PHOTOGRAPHY Marco Lavit

56–63 **OUTWARD BOUND**
COBS Year-Round Micro Cabins | Colorado Building Workshop || coloradobuildingworkshop.com
LOCATION Colorado, United States
COMPLETED 2016
AREA 300 ft² (27.8 m²)
PHOTOGRAPHY Jesse Kuroiwa

64–69 **PLATFORM OF DREAMS**
Dream/Dive Platform | Studio North || studionorth.ca
LOCATION Bobs Lake, Ontario, Canada
COMPLETED 2015
AREA 64 ft² (6 m²)
PHOTOGRAPHY Studio North

70–75 **DUTCH HOMAGE**
Thoreau's Cabin | cc-studio || cc-studio.nl
LOCATION Utrecht, the Netherlands
COMPLETED 2013
AREA 377 ft² (35 m²)
PHOTOGRAPHY John Lewis Marshall

78–87 **A WINNING SHELTER**
DublDom Kandalaksha | BIO-Architects || bio-architects.com
LOCATION Kandalaksha, Russia
COMPLETED 2018
AREA 344 ft² (32 m²)
PHOTOGRAPHY Artem Lasovsky, Galina Latushko, Ivan Ovchinnikov

88–93 **TRADITIONAL MEETS MODERN**
A Barn | OPA Form || opaform.no
LOCATION Myrkdalen, Norway
COMPLETED 2016
AREA 269 ft² (25 m²)
PHOTOGRAPHY Marina Bauer, Espen Folgerø, Rune Saevig

94–101 **BLENDING IN**
Alpine Shelter "Bivak II na Jezerih" | AO Jesenice || anzecokl.com
LOCATION Triglav National Park, Slovenia
COMPLETED 2016
AREA 97 ft² (9 m²)
PHOTOGRAPHY Anze Cokl

102–8 **TAKING IN THE VIEW**
Alpine Shelter Skuta | OFIS Architects || ofis-a.si
LOCATION Skuta Mountain, Slovenia
COMPLETED 2016
AREA 323 ft² (30 m²)
PHOTOGRAPHY Anze Cokl, Andrej Gregoric, Janez Martincic

110–17 **EXTREME SHELTER**
Kanin Winter Cabin | OFIS Architects || ofis-a.si
LOCATION Mount Kanin, Slovenia
COMPLETED 2016
AREA 104 ft² (9.7 m²)
PHOTOGRAPHY Ales Gregoric, Janez Martincic

118–25 **SNOWBOARDERS' RETREAT**
Whistler Cabin | Scott and Scott Architects || scottandscott.ca
LOCATION Whistler, British Columbia, Canada
COMPLETED 2016
AREA 1,900 ft² (176.5 m²)
PHOTOGRAPHY Scott and Scott Architects

126–31 **MINIMUM EXISTENCE**
Antoine | Daniel Zamarbide (BUREAU) with Leopold Banchini Architects || bureau.ac
LOCATION Verbier, Switzerland
COMPLETED 2014
AREA 43 ft² (4 m²)
PHOTOGRAPHY Dylan Perrenoud

134–39 **INTO THE WILD**
Ark-Shelter | Ark-shelter Studio || ark-shelter.com
LOCATION Kysuce, Slovakia
COMPLETED 2018
AREA 430.6 ft² (40 m²)
PHOTOGRAPHY BoysPlayNice

140–47 **PITCHED TO PERFECTION**
Folly | Cohesion Studio || thecohesionstudio.com
LOCATION Joshua Tree, United States
COMPLETED 2018
AREA 900 ft² (83.6 m²)
PHOTOGRAPHY Sam Frost Photography

148–55 **LEGENDARY ACCOMMODATION**
Arthur's Cave | Miller Kendrick Architects || millerkendrick.co.uk
LOCATION Castell y Bere, Wales, United Kingdom
COMPLETED 2017
AREA 134.5 ft² (12.5 m²)
PHOTOGRAPHY Paul Miller

156–59 **BENEATH THE WINGS OF CONDORS**
Shelter for the Wanderer | Hans Kubat Sarria Arquitecto || kubathans.wixsite.com/hkubatarquitecto
LOCATION Valley of the Condors, Chile
COMPLETED 2016
AREA 425 ft² (39.5 m²)
PHOTOGRAPHY Hans Kubat Sarria

Third reprint 2022
The Images Publishing Group Reference Number: 1683

First published in Australia in 2019 by
The Images Publishing Group Pty Ltd
ABN 89 059 734 431

OFFICES

Australia
Waterman Business Centre
Suite 64, Level 2 UL40
1341 Dandenong Road,
Chadstone, VIC 3148
Tel: +61 3 8564 8122

United States
6 West 18th Street 4B
New York, NY 10011
United States
Tel: +1 212 645 1111

Shanghai
6F, Building C, 838 Guangji Road
Hongkou District, Shanghai 200434
China
Tel: +86 021 31260822

books@imagespublishing.com
www.imagespublishing.com

All photography is attributed in the Project Credits on pages 298–300 unless otherwise noted. Pages 2, 20, 21: Matthew Carbone (BIG-Bjarke Ingels Group, Klein A45); Pages 4, 10: Will Scott Photography (De Rosee Sa, Woodland Cabin); Page 6: Anders Hviid and Mark Seelen (Vipp A/S, Vipp Shelter); Page 13: Dylan Minchenberg (CABN, CABN "Jude"); Page 15: Atelier LAVIT (Atelier LAVIT, ORIGIN Tree House); Pages 18–19: Andrej Gregoric (OFIS Architects, Alpine Shelter Skuta); Page 22: Studio North (Studio North, Dream/Dive Platform); Pages 24–25, 76–77, 132–33, 172–73, 224–25, 270–71, and endpapers: iStockphoto.

NATIONAL LIBRARY OF AUSTRALIA
A catalogue record for this book is available from the National Library of Australia

Title: Cabins: Escape to Nature
Author: Damon Hayes Couture [Introduction]
ISBN: 9781864708332

Printed on 150gsm GalerieArt Matt paper by DZS Grafik (Slovenia)

FSC www.fsc.org MIX Paper from responsible sources FSC® C106600

IMAGES has included on its website a page for special notices in relation to this and our other publications.
Please visit www.imagespublishing.com